*More than two centuries ago, the Fou...   )-
cedure for Congress to follow in the event   'f
Executive. That process is impeachment. I .... deceit
and disregard for the Constitution that we ...ave witnessed on the part of the
President over the past seven years, Congressman Kucinich's initiation of this
process is neither fanciful nor futile, neither vengeful nor vindictive; it is the sober
fulfillment of his sworn duty as a Congressman to follow the law without regard
to personal consequence and misguided political stratagem. It is, quite simply,
an act of patriotism.*

—**Elizabeth de la Vega**, Former Federal Prosecutor
and author of *United States v. George W. Bush et. al.*

*This collection of impeachable offenses should be viewed as a sampling of
the crimes and abuses of President George W. Bush and his subordinates. Bush
has had many accomplices — first and foremost Vice President Cheney. But our
Founders created a single executive precisely so that we could hold that one person accountable for the actions of the executive branch. It is high time we did
so, and millions of Americans will be urging their representatives to support the
effort being led by Congressman Kucinich.*

*These articles establish, and hearings would establish further, that President
Bush was 'the decider' behind countless abuses of power. And, of course, his
public comments have time and again advertised his indifference to the laws he
is violating. Not only does overwhelming evidence show us that Bush knew his
claims about WMDs to be false, but the president has shown us that he consid-
ers the question of truth or falsehood to be laughably irrelevant. When Diane
Sawyer asked Bush why he had claimed with such certainty that there were so
many weapons in Iraq, he replied: "What's the difference? The possibility that
[Saddam] could acquire weapons, If he were to acquire weapons, he would be
the danger."*

*What's the difference? Hundreds of thousands of corpses and a fatal blow to
the rule of law among nations. That's the difference. Unless we remove impeachment from the Constitution by failing to exercise it, in which case truth will no
longer matter any more than justice or peace.*

— **David Swanson**, creator of ImpeachCheney.org, Washington
Director of Democrats.com and co-founder of the AfterDowningStreet.org.

Overload is the main problem—I call it outrage fatigue. The sheer multitude, not to mention magnitude, of impeachable offenses tends to dull the senses. The opportunity to dig into just one or two provided some space and focused the mind.

At the same time, the deeper one digs, the more unimaginable the dirt that comes up. Earlier, I had not taken the time to sift through the abundant evidence of the unconscionable ways in which George Bush and George Tenet teamed up—including, in Tenet's case, lying under oath—to stave off charges of misfeasance/malfeasance before the attacks on 9/11.

The Founders pledged their lives, their fortunes, and their sacred honor to create a system in which we could protect ourselves from unbridled power. Today, we cannot let a 21st Century string of abuses and usurpations stand without challenge.

But the experience of the past several years shows that there is a very high hurdle in our way: no Common Sense. I refer, of course, to the courageous independent journalism of the likes of Tom Paine who stirred the innate dignity of Americans toward sacrifice for independence and freedom. Tom Paine would be horrified to see what has become of his profession today—with browbeaten journalists and former general officers doing the bidding of the corporations that own/pay them.

In my view, impeachment proceedings are essential to:

• Reestablish the separation of powers in our Constitution as a check on the so-called unitary executive';
• Prevent a budding—and catastrophic—US attack on Iran by exposing it as yet another war of aggression against a country posing no threat to the US;
• Call attention to the blood already drained from our civil liberties and stanch the bleeding.

Impeachment proceedings may be the only way to force the captive media to inform normal citizens about what has been going on in our country. Thomas Jefferson underscored the importance of this when he said: "Whenever the people are well informed, they can be trusted with their own government."

—**Ray McGovern**; former Army officer and CIA analyst; co-founder, Veteran Intelligence Professionals for Sanity

President Bush, Cheney and other US officials have violated numerous domestic and international laws governing crime of aggression, war crime, torture, etc., and they should be not only impeached by the US Congress but also be prosecuted by a special prosecutor, to the full extent of the law before or after impeachment. That is the best way to uphold the US Constitution and the rule of law at home and abroad.

—**John Kim**, Esq., Attorney;
author of *The Crime of Aggression Against Iraq*

The breadth of impeachable offenses committed by the Bush/Cheney administration is likely unparalleled in our nation's history. Equally unparalleled, and in many cases even more alarming and outrageous, is the lack of accountability brought to the perpetrators of these High Crimes and Misdemeanors. It is the Constitutional duty of members of Congress—members from any political party—to bring such accountability, particularly when the list of crimes began with the very acts that brought this administration into office during their elections, and right up through today when the same sort of crimes continue, and are in place to try and affect our next Presidential Election.

This is not about politics, it's about the Constitutional duty of Congress. If a line in the sand is not drawn immediately and clearly in the face of such corruption and disdain for our American values, such as the Rule of Law, the historical bar for criminality in our Executive Branch will have been forever lowered, no matter who happens to serve in the White House in the future.

—**Brad Friedman**, creator/ editor of The Brad Blog,
and co-founder of the watchdog organization VelvetRevolution.us.

★

"I have provided the legal architecture and evidence for a trial to prosecute the President for murder. My book lends credence to a powerful case for impeachment laid out persuasively by Congressman Dennis Kucinich's 35 Articles of Impeachment."

— **Vincent Bugliosi**, Former District Attorney,
author of *The Prosecution of George W. Bush for Murder*

THE 35 ARTICLES OF IMPEACHMENT AND THE CASE FOR PROSECUTING GEORGE W. BUSH

THE 35 ARTICLES OF IMPEACHMENT

AND THE CASE FOR

PROSECUTING

GEORGE W. BUSH

**The full text of
Congressman Dennis Kucinich's
35 Articles of Impeachment**

**A list of the criminal violations
in the Articles, produced by
Elizabeth de la Vega**

**An original introduction by
David Swanson**

The 35 Articles of Impeachment and the Case for Prosecuting George W. Bush
by Congressman Dennis Kucinich
is in the public domain as part
of the Congressional Record,
June 09, 2008

Kucinich, the Resolution, and the Prosecution of Impeachable Crimes
© 2008 by David Swanson

Articles of Impeachment chart © 2008 by Elizabeth de la Vega
and originally published by The Public Record (pubrecord.org)

To prevent confusion, the publisher retained the conventions of the
Congressional Record in reproduction of Impeachment Articles. But the
publisher did check and supplement the various source notes provided by
Mr. Kucinich and Mr. Swanson for accuracy and availability online.

ISBN for trade edition: 978-1-932595-42-0

A Feral House Original Paperback
www.FeralHouse.com

Design by Sean Tejaratchi

For further information about Feral House and related titles,
please see www.FeralHouse.com

10 9 8 7 6 5 4 3 2 1

TABLE OF CONTENTS

Kucinich, the Resolution, and the Prosecution of Impeachable Crimes

By David Swanson

When former president George W. Bush and former Vice President Dick Cheney are finally hauled into court, their first line of defense is likely to be, "We served the American people, whose representatives chose not to impeach us." If, on the other hand, they are impeached, even after having left office, the likelihood of prosecution and of successful prosecution will increase dramatically. Impeachment after January 2009 would not remove them from office, but could cut off their public pensions and bar them from ever holding any public office again. Those would be trivial results, but the primary impact of impeachment would be to establish for future presidents and vice presidents that there is a penalty to be paid for violating the law or abusing power.

For the penalty to include prison time will require prosecution at the federal, state, or local level, or in a foreign country or international court. The possibilities for prosecution are more diverse and more likely than for impeachment. While Congress has not yet aided the cause of prosecution by impeaching, Dennis Kucinich has done so by drafting an extensive indictment in the form of the 35 articles of impeachment contained in this book.

On the evening of June 9, 2008, Congressman Kucinich of Cleveland, Ohio, had been working many hours without a break or a bite to eat, and I would have assumed that he was near the point of collapse had I not worked with him before. But it was Dennis, and he grabbed a thick sheaf of paper from the printer, and continued making changes as he headed to the floor of the House of Representatives, and read aloud, for nearly six hours, 35 Articles of Impeachment against President George W. Bush. The impeachment news flashed across the internet and through the radio waves, and C-Span's viewership soared. Two days later, after the clerk of the House had read the entire resolution (H. Res. 1258) aloud again, the full House voted to send it to the House Judiciary Committee, to be considered or ignored, as that committee's chairman or his party's leader saw fit.

Kucinich had introduced articles of impeachment against Vice President Dick Cheney, in April 2007, and reintroduced them to force a vote in November '07 that sent them to committee. When Dennis introduced the 35 articles of impeachment against Bush in June 2008, he threatened to come back with 60 articles in July if no action had yet been taken. That didn't happen, but Kucinich did go back to the floor in July and forced a vote on a single article of impeachment against Bush related to the invasion of Iraq, the issue Kucinich had focused on above all others.

At that point Nancy Pelosi, Speaker of the House, told John Conyers, Chairman of the Judiciary Committee, to hold a hearing at which Kucinich could present his case for impeachment, but to announce in advance that no actual impeachment proceedings would follow the hearing, no matter what was heard there. The hearing was held on July 25th, and Kucinich and other members of Congress, former members of Congress, former prosecutors, and other experts argued for impeachment, many of them drawing on the arguments made in Kucinich's 35 articles. The hearing, like Kucinich's reading of his articles, took six hours, and was probably the most devastating indictment of a sitting president and vice president in the history of the nation. The corporate media almost completely ignored it. A couple of weeks later, some concerned citizens caught up with Pelosi, who was touring the country to sell her new book, and asked for her opinion of Kucinich's articles of impeachment. She replied that she had not yet read them.

If you find this book valuable and believe that Speaker Pelosi can't possibly read it too many times, you can mail your copy along with a personal note to:

Nancy Pelosi
450 Golden Gate Ave. — 14th Floor
San Francisco, CA 94102

as in Kucinich's articles, but it had been made in print in 2005 by a group called the International Commission of Inquiry on Crimes Against Humanity Committed by the Bush Administration of the United States, as well as by Congressman Conyers and his staff in a book written in 2005, and in books in 2006 by the Center for Constitutional Rights, Dave Lindorff and Barbara Olshansky, Elizabeth Holtzman and Cynthia L. Cooper, and Dennis Loo and Peter Phillips, among others.

A plausible ground for impeachment can be found in the record of just about every past US president, at least with the benefit of evidence that has emerged since their terms in office; but none of them come anywhere close to the record documented in Kucinich's 35 Articles. Bush and Cheney have outdone all past presidents and vice presidents combined in volume and degree of abuses of power. The 35 Articles could quite easily become 60 or more.

Bush broke more laws on some single days than some of his predecessors did in their entire terms in office. January 31, 2003, stands out in my mind. That was when Bush met with British Prime Minister Tony Blair in the White House and proposed possible ways to provoke Saddam Hussein into an attack, which included the painting of US airplanes with United Nations colors and trying to get them shot at. Bush also proposed assassinating Hussein. He also promised Blair that he would try to get the United Nations to legalize the coming invasion, the same day the National Security Agency (NSA) launched a campaign to bug the phones and emails of key members of the U.N. Security Council.

When Bush and Blair finished their private chat, they held a press conference at which they professed not to have decided on war, to continue working for peace, and to be worried about the imminent threat from Iraq to the American people. They claimed that Iraq possessed "weapons of mass destruction" and had links to al Qaeda and — as Bush implied but avoided explicitly stating — to the attacks of September 11, 2001. They also claimed to already have U.N. authorization for launching an attack on Iraq. At this time the US military was already engaging in bombing runs over Iraq, and redeploying troops — including to newly-constructed bases — all in preparation for an invasion of Iraq, and all with money that had not been appropriated for these purposes.

Half the crimes in the above paragraph did not make the cut in the 35 articles, and yet Iraq cast such a shadow that misdeeds in other parts of the world didn't make the list at all. Who recalls the bizarre incident in which the United States kidnapped and imprisoned the president of Haiti? Who's suffering from too much scandal fatigue to focus on the secret US funding and assistance to an attempted coup against the president of Venezuela? What about the US encouragement and aid to Israel's bombing of civilian targets in Lebanon? President Bush issued an Executive Order on July 17, 2007, that authorized the Treasury Department to seize the assets of American citizens on the basis of a non-judicial process that denies them their Fifth Amendment rights, but how can we get excited about that when the things Bush did on most other days were worse?

A law called the Hatch Act bars the use of federal resources for partisan politics, and prohibits partisan political events and other partisan efforts during work hours at federal government facilities, but Karl Rove routinely worked on partisan politics out of the White House and held over 100 illegal events in the Old Executive Office Building and at a variety of government agencies. The First Amendment bans state religion, and yet Bush and gang used numerous departments of the government to promote Christianity, in violation of a variety of laws. In fact, you can pick just about any department answering to the president and find that Bush and/or Cheney (usually Cheney) exercised an unprecedented degree of control over it, reversed the decisions of the head of the department, censored the reports of the staff, and imposed policies in violation of laws.

Take the Environmental Protection Agency (EPA) as an example that didn't find its way into the 35 articles. In July 2008, former EPA official Jason Burnett blew the whistle on Dick Cheney, reporting that Cheney's office had pushed successfully to have "any discussion of the human health consequences of climate change" removed from testimony that Julie Gerberding, director of the Center for Disease Control had presented to Congress in 2007. Under administrator Stephen Johnson, the EPA consistently took its orders from Cheney and Bush, and pressured scientists to make their findings conform to White House demands.

In August 2003 the Bush Administration denied a petition to regulate C02 emissions from motor vehicles by deciding that CO^2 was not a pollutant under the Clean Air Act. In April 2007 the US Supreme Court overruled that determination. The EPA then conducted an extensive investigation involving 60 to 70 staff who concluded that "CO^2 emissions endanger both human health and welfare." These findings were submitted to the White House, after which work on the required regulations was effectively delayed for the remainder of the Cheney-Bush presidency.

Johnson's EPA set ozone pollution limits at unhealthy levels after rejecting the conclusions of its own scientists, and then weakened those limits further after a late-night intervention by Bush on the eve of announcing the new standards. And Johnson and the EPA stonewalled Congress, refusing to produce subpoenaed documents, leading top senators and Congress members to pathetically ask Johnson to resign, which of course he did not do, as he was merely following orders from Cheney and Bush whom Pelosi had promised never to impeach.

A close look at Bush and Cheney's handling of the economy might find impeachable offenses as well, ranging from protection of (rather than from) predatory mortgage lenders, neglect of a foreclosure crisis, and abuses such as the incident in March 2008 when Bush and his Treasury Secretary transferred a mountain of public money to J.P. Morgan/Chase via the Federal Reserve, in order to induce J.P. Morgan/Chase to assume the liabilities and assets of Bear Stearns and Company at a price not determined in the free market or via public bidding, in violation of the limitations expressly set forth in the Federal Reserve Act.

Most of the 35 Articles below address Bush, Cheney, and Bush's other subordinates, and rightly so. The framers of the Constitution chose a single executive in order to hold him (or her) accountable for the entire branch of government. But articles focused on Cheney would have added more crimes to the list. The resolution that Kucinich introduced in April 2007 did not attempt comprehensive coverage. It included only three Articles of Impeachment, alleging that Cheney had misled the Congress and the public about "weapons of mass destruction" and about ties to al Qaeda, and had threatened an aggressive war on Iran. Cheney had also personally profited financially from the invasion and occupation of Iraq, via no-bid contracts that he awarded to a company still paying him "deferred compensation."

And, of course, more crimes and abuses have emerged since July 2008, including evidence of partisan hiring practices at the Justice Department, and more evidence has emerged in support of the allegations found in the 35 articles, including evidence of war lies reported in Ron Suskind's *The Way of the World*. It is a good bet that yet more evidence will continue to be made public in the coming months and years.

Again, impeachment will remain possible, even with Bush and Cheney out of office. Penalties that can be imposed include removal of pension and barring from ever again holding public office. Civil and criminal prosecution will be far more likely with Bush and Cheney and their subordinates out of office. Whether impeachment or prosecution or other major steps to reform our political system occur will largely not be determined by the outcomes of elections, and the question of whether they occur is more important than the outcomes of elections.

I agree with George Mason's analysis of our system of government when he said on July 20, 1787, that "No point is of more importance than that the right of impeachment should be continued. Shall any man be above Justice? Above all shall that man be above it, who can commit the most extensive injustice?"

Impeachment has been used far more routinely through American history than most people realize. The history of impeachment is very well told by John Nichols in his book, *The Genius of Impeachment: The Founders' Cure for Royalism*. Impeachment proceedings have been initiated in the House 62 times, and 17 people have been impeached. Thirteen of those have been federal judges, one a secretary of war, one a senator, and two presidents. Seven individuals have subsequently been convicted in a trial in the US Senate, all of them federal judges.

But that's not the half of it. Impeachment often achieves its purpose of preserving our democratic rights short of actually arriving at a majority House vote for impeachment. Richard Nixon was never impeached, but he rightly resigned from the presidency. Harry Truman was never impeached, but he ceased the abuses of power for which Congress Members were pushing to impeach him and which the Supreme Court rapidly ruled against (during "war time" to boot). Attorney General Alberto Gonzales was never impeached, but there was a major push in Congress to impeach him. Prior to summer recess 2007, there were 32 Congress members who had cosponsored a resolution calling for impeachment hearings to begin. Many more pledged to sign on when Congress returned in the fall, but before that occurred, Gonzales announced his resignation.

Our Constitution was written as Edmund Burke was leading the impeachment of Warren Hastings in England—an effort that did not achieve impeachment but did restore democratic checks on power. American colonies, too, impeached governors and justices. In recent years, the British Parliament saw an active effort to impeach Prime Minister Tony Blair, which weakened his power. Impeachments went on in nations all over the world during the Cheney-Bush era, and a threat of impeachment led Pakistan's President Pervez Musharraf to resign.

While only two US presidents, Bill Clinton and Andrew Johnson, have been impeached, and neither one of them convicted in the Senate, articles of impeachment have also been filed in the House against presidents Tyler, Cleveland, Hoover, Truman, Nixon, Reagan, Bush Sr., and Bush Jr. That's a total of 10 out of 43 presidents, or 23 percent. Some of these cases involved serious threats of impeachment, and others involved one or a dozen defenders of our rights in Congress going up against Congressional leaders intent on ignoring them.

Since polling began, the least popular president on record is Bush Jr., but both Truman and Nixon came close. Both were unpopular for seizing too much power. In both cases, Congress began steps toward impeachment. In both cases, abuses of power were checked. Neither Nixon nor Truman, however, ever held as much unconstitutional power as did the real all-time leader in unpopularity: Dick Cheney.

Even this expanded list of past impeachments leaves out most of the history of impeachment movements, which have pushed from the local level up, both successfully and unsuccessfully, for the impeachment of officials in Washington. One of the judges successfully impeached and convicted was impeached after a state legislature petitioned the House to impeach him, and another after an individual petitioned the House. The Jefferson Manual, a book of rules that Thomas Jefferson originally wrote for the Senate but which is now used by the House, and which has been much added to since Jefferson's day, includes procedures by which individuals and state and local governments have in the past petitioned, and can in the future petition, the House to impeach. Such petitions are not binding, but can influence Congress when Congress is willing to be influenced.

Impeachment has been a path to electoral success throughout US history. After the Whigs attempted to impeach Tyler, they picked up seven seats, and Tyler left politics. Weeks after he lobbied for Johnson's impeachment, Grant was nominated for president. Lincoln had pushed toward the impeachment of Polk without introducing actual articles. He, too, was elected president. Keith Ellison, who introduced a resolution to impeach Bush and Cheney into the Minnesota state legislature, was elected to Congress in 2006, where he did very little to support impeachment. After the Republicans pursued impeachment of Truman and won what they wanted (and the nation needed) from the Supreme Court, they won in the next elections. After Nixon resigned, the Democrats won the White House and picked up 4 seats in the Senate and 49 (yes, 49!) in the House. Even during and following the unpopular impeachment of Clinton (an impeachment the public was overwhelmingly opposed to), the Republicans held onto majorities in both houses and lost very few seats. They also had the pleasure of watching Al Gore campaign for president while pretending he was never close to Bill Clinton and picking the unpopular Joe Lieberman, an advocate for Clinton's impeachment, as his running mate. On the other hand, when Democrats chose not to pursue impeachment of Reagan for Iran-Contra, so that they could win the next elections, the result was that they lost the next elections.

Proposals to impeach Bush were almost always greeted by Congress members with horrified shouts of "But we wouldn't want a President Cheney!" The greatest insurance against impeachment was an unpopular and frightening vice president. Never mind that Cheney's unpopularity would have hurt his own party had he been made president. Never mind that impeachment is a process that often accomplishes great things short of getting to impeachment, much less removal from office. Never mind that if Bush could be impeached, Cheney certainly could too. It didn't matter By failing to impeach Bush and Cheney we have established for future presidents and vice presidents that they can break the law without expecting to be impeached.

Congress members and their staffers believed that the Clinton impeachment had ruined impeachment for good. There were perfectly good reasons to impeach Bill Clinton, but he was impeached in an absurd bad-faith witch hunt that made a mockery of our entire system of government.

In March 2006, the *Wall Street Journal* did—for one day—what most media outlets never did: cover the movement to impeach Bush and Cheney. While most polling companies refused to ever poll on the question, even for cold hard cash, Zogby had released a poll in November 2005 that we at After Downing Street and Democrats.com had commissioned. The *Wall Street Journal* led off with a graphic showing the results of that poll and those of a 1998 poll on impeaching Clinton. The same pollster had conducted both polls and asked very similar questions. Both polls were conducted among "likely voters." The results showed that 27 percent favored impeachment for Clinton and 51 percent for Bush. That would have been an impressive gap even without the contrasting media attention. The impeachment of Clinton was promoted in saturation coverage night-and-day for months, with newspapers editorializing in support of it. The impeachment of Bush was absolutely unheard of and unmentionable in US corporate media.

The *Wall Street Journal* did print that one article, but—tellingly—the article was written exactly as if the reporter had not seen the graphic at the top and was unaware of the poll results. "Democratic Party leaders," she wrote, were "keeping their distance from impeachment talk. They remember how the effort boomeranged on Republicans in the 1998 midterm elections." Of course, that boomerang was minimal (the Republicans lost five seats and held the majority), but look at those poll results again. The voters didn't want Clinton impeached, and did want Bush impeached. So, why in the world would voter opposition to the former suggest that there would be voter opposition to the latter?

From Impeachment to Prosecution

To the credit of the American people, the impeachment movement continued to grow, but off the radar of the Wall Street Journal. The movement educated the public, influenced elections, and made lies about Iran a lot harder to swallow than lies about Iraq had been. And now its focus is shifting from Congress to courts, from impeachment to prosecution. Not all impeachable offenses are crimes, and not all crimes are impeachable offenses, but there are quite a few crimes in Kucinich's 35 articles. Following this introduction is a list of the crimes alleged. The list was drawn up by Elizabeth de la Vega, a former federal prosecutor and the author of *United States v. George W. Bush et al.*, a brilliant book that depicts a presentation to a grand jury charging Bush and gang with defrauding the nation into war.

Now, according to Fox News, the only reason any of us ever favored impeachment was because we hated Bush and Cheney and couldn't beat them at the ballot box (on the latter point, see Articles XXVIII and XXIX below). Having failed, at least so far, at impeachment, pursuing prosecution (even after an election has solved all our problems or at least altered them) must surely be driven by nothing other than hatred, right?

Wrong. If I thought we could deter future presidents and vice presidents from abusing power by giving Cheney and Bush immunity for life, that is exactly what I would propose we do. I would advocate for any deterrent effect. I take the matter this seriously because we are preparing to hand what Michael Goldfarb, Deputy Communications Director for presidential candidate John McCain, approvingly calls "near dictatorial power" to every future president and vice president at a moment in history in which the twin dangers of global warming and nuclear war threaten us far more seriously than has any nation with which ours has ever clashed.

While some have talked of hanging Bush and Cheney after the manner of punishment we imposed on German and Japanese war criminals, I am adamantly opposed to the possibility of imposing the death penalty on anyone, no matter what they are convicted of, because it has been shown to encourage violence rather than to deter it. Future presidents are not more likely to refrain from abusing power if they might be executed than if they might be imprisoned for life. If they are imprisoned for life, they can express their regrets in ways that their successors can understand.

As I write this two months prior to the 2008 elections, we may have an honest and verifiable election in November, but it's difficult to see how that is possible. And though we may elect a president and vice president who abide fully by the Constitution, the treaties our nation has ratified, and the laws that are on the books, that's very unlikely.

In a December 31, 2007, editorial, the *New York Times* faulted Bush and Cheney for kidnapping innocent people, denying justice to prisoners, torturing, murdering, circumventing US and international law, spying in violation of the Fourth Amendment, and basing their actions on "imperial fantasies." If the editorial had been about robbing a liquor store or killing a small number of people or stealing a small amount of money or torturing a single child, then the writers at the *New York Times* would have demanded immediate prosecution and incarceration. In this case they demanded that we sit back and hope the next president and vice president will be better. How does that deter future crimes?

We can announce new policies, pass new legislation, amend the Constitution. We can shift power to the Congress, and clean up our electoral system to allow true representation of the people in the Congress. We can shift our resources from the military to peaceful enterprises. We can eliminate secret government and create total transparency. We can perfect the brilliant cutting-edge democratic system that our nation created over two centuries ago and has done little to update since. We can put an end to plutocracy, reclaim our airwaves, ban war propaganda, and develop different public attitudes toward those 95.5 percent of people in the world who are not Americans. And so we should. But all that would not be sufficient to chain the dogs of war. Exquisite laws and enlightened public attitudes are of no use at all as long as presidents and vice presidents suffer no penalty for disobeying them, and in fact benefit politically and financially.

During the Democratic primaries, Senator Obama said he'd have his attorney general look into the possibility that Bush and Cheney had committed crimes, but that as far as he knew they hadn't committed any. He later voted to give telecom companies immunity for cooperating with some of the crimes. In early September Joe Biden said that he, too, didn't know of any crimes that had been committed, but that an Obama-Biden administration would look into the question. He also promised a justice department that would no longer commit crimes. The day after Biden made these remarks, he went on TV to insist that an Obama-Biden administration has no intention of prosecuting Bush and Cheney.

There's a much more serious potential roadblock to domestic criminal prosecution than Barack Obama's (and, of course, John McCain's) belief that Bush and Cheney's crimes should be hushed up, namely the possibility that Bush will issue blanket pardons of anyone who engaged in crimes he authorized, including himself. Without admitting that Bush or anyone else has committed any crimes, Obama or McCain could take a position against any president, himself included, ever pardoning anyone for a crime that the president authorizes. A focus on pardons at least begins to limit the power of the individual holding all the power. Congress, unless it is restored to power, serves — at best — as just more people lobbying the president.

Now, blanket pardons or self-pardons could be challenged. There may be local and state and civil prosecutions possible despite pardons and strengthened by pardons. And prosecution by a foreign country or the International Criminal Court (ICC) is a possibility as well. With Obama and Biden suggesting they will "investigate" whether any crimes have been committed, there is no reason that they could not. That commitment is a second demand that we can make of the candidates for president or the president elect.

On the subject of local and state prosecutions, *The Prosecution of George W. Bush for Murder* by Vincent Bugliosi argues that state and local prosecutors have jurisdiction to prosecute Bush for the murder of US soldiers from their states and counties who died in Iraq. We need to identify or elect courageous prosecutors and pair them up with gold star families.

Some have expressed concern that when Cheney and Bush leave office they will destroy lots of evidence of their crimes. I do not share this concern, because they already have destroyed lots of such evidence, and yet more than enough such evidence is in the public realm. And there is something that cannot be destroyed: the many potential whistleblowers who have been keeping their mouths shut. We should not be relying on Congress. We should not be funneling our money through electoral campaigns and into TV ads on television networks that are destroying our country. We should be establishing a whistleblower protection fund that can guarantee financial security and legal defense to those considering blowing the whistle on their superiors.

There are also a variety of ways in which citizens can file suit. My friend John Bonifaz served as attorney on a lawsuit against the President before the invasion of Iraq on behalf of Congress members (including Kucinich) and military families claiming an invasion would be unconstitutional without a proper congressional declaration of war. John consulted in 2007 with a professor at Rutgers University, who worked up a case with his students for a full year, and in 2008 filed it in Federal District Court in Newark, New Jersey. The Complaint, filed on behalf of a number of peace groups, seeks a Declaratory Judgment that the President's decision to launch a preemptive war against a sovereign nation in 2003 violated Article I, Section 8 of the United States Constitution, which assigns to Congress the power to Declare War. Every peace and justice group in the country should be working with lawyers, choosing their favorite Cheney-Bush crime, and filing a suit, the point being to change the public conversation until we reach the point that a prosecutor will act.

There is also a procedure called Qui Tam found in the Federal False Claims Act that allows individual citizens to sue if the government spends money fraudulently, and to receive a percentage of any funds recovered. Such a suit could conceivable be filed, or perhaps hundreds of such suits could be filed, against government officials, including Dick Cheney, who set up illegal contracts with Halliburton and other corporations, including contracts to spend in Iraq funding that had been legally appropriated for Afghanistan.

Prosecution is also possible in foreign nations. In May 2008 in Milano, Italy, 25 CIA agents and an Air Force colonel went on trial in absentia for kidnapping a man on an Italian street and renditioning him to Egypt to be tortured. The victim's wife testified for over six hours. A newspaper report read:

> Nabila at first rebuffed prosecutors' requests to describe the torture her husband had recounted, saying she didn't want to talk about it. Advised by prosecutors that she had no choice, she tearfully proceeded: "He was tied up like he was being crucified. He was beaten up, especially around his ears. He was subject to electroshocks to many body parts."
> "To his genitals?' the prosecutors asked.
> "Yes,' she replied."

The judge said that the current and immediate past prime ministers of Italy would be required to testify during the trial.

Foreign victims can also sue in US courts. Also in May 2008, an Iraqi sued US contractors for torture. Emad al-Janabi's federal lawsuit was filed in Los Angeles and claimed that employees of CACI International Inc. and L-3 Communications punched him, slammed him into walls, hung him from a bed frame and kept him naked and handcuffed in his cell. In July, three more Iraqis and a Jordanian who had been held and tortured in Abu Ghraib for years before being released without charges filed similar suits. Alleged methods of torture by the US contractors included: electric shock, beatings, depriving of food and sleep, threatening with dogs, stripping naked, forcibly shaving, choking, being forced to witness murder, pouring feces on, holding down and sodomizing (a 14-year-old boy) with a toothbrush, being paraded naked before other prisoners, forcing to consume so much water that you vomit blood and faint, and tying a plastic line around your penis to prevent urination.

And on August 15, 2008, the Second Circuit Court of Appeals in New York announced that it would hear the case against the United States of Canadian victim of US torture Maher Arar. His suit names, among others, former Attorney General John Ashcroft, former Deputy Attorney General Larry Thompson, and former head of "Homeland Security" Tom Ridge.

We can also work at the local level to follow the example of Brattleboro, Vt., passing ordinances making it the law that if Bush, Cheney, or key co-conspirators enter our towns they will be arrested.

And we can make citizens arrests all on our own right now. Here's how: afterdowningstreet.org/citizenarrest

Judge William Price in Iowa in July heard the case of people who had been arrested for trying to make a citizens' arrest of Karl Rove. When told what they were charged with, the judge remarked "Well, it's about time!"

And it's about time we re-established what John Adams called a government of laws and not of men. To get involved in that project, go to the website: afterdowningstreet.org and to Dennis Kucinich's website: kucinich.us.

List of Crimes

ARTICLES OF IMPEACHMENT
FOR PRESIDENT GEORGE W. BUSH

U.S. AND INTERNATIONAL VIOLATIONS ALLEGED

INTRODUCED BY REP. DENNIS KUCINICH (D. Ohio)
JUNE 09, 2008

CITE	VIOLATION	ARTICLES
U.S. Constitution Art. II, Sec. 1 Oath of Office	"I do solemnly swear (or affirm) that I will faithfully execute the office of President of the United States, and will to the best of my ability, preserve, protect and defend the Constitution of the United States."	One thru Thirty-five
U.S. Constitution, Art. II, Sec. 3	"[The President] shall take care that the laws be faithfully executed."	One thru Thirty-five
Title 18, U.S. Code, Sec. 2	"(a)Whoever commits an offense against the U. S. or aids, abets, counsels, commands, induces or procures its commission [and/or] (b)willfully causes an act to be done which if directly performed by him or another would be an offense against the U.S., is punishable as a principal."	One thru Thirty-five
Covert Propaganda Prohibition included in all Congressional Appropriation Legislation	Prohibits use of any appropriated funds "for propaganda purposes, and for the preparation, distribution or use of any kit, pamphlet, booklet, publication, radio, television or film presentation designed to support or defeat legislation pending before the Congress, except in presentation to the Congress itself."	One thru Four; Ten; Thirty
Title 18, U.S. Code, Sec. 371 [Conspiracy to Defraud the United States]	Prohibits conspiring to use any form of fraud in an effort to impair or obstruct the function of a U.S. Government branch or agency.	One thru Six; Ten thru Thirteen; Sixteen; Twenty-one; Twenty-two; Thirty; Thirty-two; Thirty-five

ARTICLES OF IMPEACHMENT
FOR PRESIDENT GEORGE W. BUSH

U.S. AND INTERNATIONAL VIOLATIONS ALLEGED

INTRODUCED BY REP. DENNIS KUCINICH (D. Ohio)
JUNE 09, 2008

Title 18, U.S. Code, Secs. 1341, 1346	Prohibit using mail and wire communications to further a scheme to defraud the public of its right to the honest services of its public officials via false pretenses, representations, promises and material omissions.	One thru Four; Ten; Twenty-one; Thirty; Thirty-two; Thirty-five
U.S. Constitution Art. I, Sec. 9	"No Money shall be drawn from the Treasury, but in Consequence of Appropriations made by Law…"	Five
U.S. Constitution Art. I, Sec. 8	"[Congress shall have the power] to declare War…"	Five thru Seven
War Powers Act of 1973, Sec. 9(d)(1)	"Nothing in this joint resolution—is intended to alter the constitutional authority of the Congress or of the President…"	Five thru Seven
JRes 114, Sec. 3	"[In connection with the exercise of authority to use force, the President shall advise Congress of his determination] that –(1) reliance by the United States on further diplomatic or other peaceful means alone either (A) will not adequately protect the national security of the U.S. against the continuing threat posed by Iraq or (B) is not likely to lead to enforcement of all relevant United Nations Security Council resolutions regarding Iraq; and (2) acting pursuant to this joint resolution is consistent with the U.S. and other countries continuing to take the necessary actions against international terrorist and terrorist organizations, including those nations, organizations, or persons who planned, authorized, committed or aided the terrorist attacks that occurred on September 11, 2001."	Five thru Seven
U.S. Constitution, Art. VI	"[A]ll Treaties made…under the Authority of the United States, shall be the Supreme Law of the Land."	Eight

ARTICLES OF IMPEACHMENT
FOR PRESIDENT GEORGE W. BUSH

U.S. AND INTERNATIONAL VIOLATIONS ALLEGED

INTRODUCED BY REP. DENNIS KUCINICH (D. Ohio)
JUNE 09, 2008

Ch. I, Art.2 UN Charter, Section 3	"[All Members shall] settle their international disputes by peaceful means in such a manner that international peace and security, and justice, are not endangered" and "4. Refrain in their international relations from the threat or use of force against ... [another state]."	Eight
Title 18, U.S. Code, Sec. 2441	"a) Whoever, [while being a national of the U.S.] commits a war crime, [shall be guilty of a felony]." "(d) [T]he term 'war crime' means any conduct-(1) defined as a grave breach in any of the international conventions at Geneva 12 August 1949, or any protocol to such convention to which the U.S. is a party."	Eight; Seventeen thru Twenty
Add'l Protocol I of 8 June, 1977 to Geneva Conventions of 12 August, Art. 85 (3) (signed by U.S.)	A "grave breach" of the Geneva Conventions includes making civilians the object of attacks.	Eight
Nat'l Defense Authorization Act for Fiscal Year 2008, Sec. 1222	"[No funds appropriated pursuant to this Act] may be obligated ...(1) To establish any military installation or base for the purpose of providing for the permanent stationing of United States Armed Forces in Iraq. (2) To exercise United States control of the oil resources of Iraq."	Eleven
Title 18, U.S. Code, Sec. 4	"Whoever, having knowledge of the actual commission of a felony cognizable by a court of the United States, conceals and does not as soon as possible make known the same to some judge or other [U.S. authority, shall be guilty of a felony.]"	Fourteen
Title 18, U.S. Code, Sec. 4	"Whoever, having knowledge of the actual commission of a felony cognizable by a court of the United States, conceals and does not as soon as possible make known the same to some judge or other [U.S. authority, shall be guilty of a felony.]"	Fourteen

ARTICLES OF IMPEACHMENT
FOR PRESIDENT GEORGE W. BUSH

U.S. AND INTERNATIONAL VIOLATIONS ALLEGED

INTRODUCED BY REP. DENNIS KUCINICH (D. Ohio)
JUNE 09, 2008

Fourth Geneva Convention	Provides that it is the responsibility of an occupying force to ensure the protection and human rights of civilians.	Fifteen
U.S. Constitution, Art. 1, Sec. 9	"The Privilege of the Writ of Habeas Corpus shall not be suspended, unless when in Cases of Rebellion or Invasion the public Safety may require it."	Seventeen
Fourth Geneva Convention, Commentary	"Every person in enemy hands…is either a prisoner of war…covered by the Third Convention, a civilian covered by the Fourth Convention, or…a member of the medical personnel of the armed forces… covered by the First Convention. There is no intermediate status; nobody in enemy hands can be outside the law."	Seventeen through Nineteen
U.S. Constitution, Fifth Amendment	No person shall be "deprived of life, liberty, or property, without due process of law…"	Seventeen
Third Geneva Convention	"No physical or mental torture, nor any other form of coercion, may be inflicted on [POWs] to secure…information of any kind whatever. [POWs] who refuse to answer may not be threatened, insulted or exposed to any unpleasant or disadvantageous treatment of any kind."	Seventeen thru Nineteen
Title 18, U.S. Code, Sec. 2340A	Prohibits torture and conspiracy to do so by U.S. nationals outside the U.S. Torture is an "act committed by a person acting under the color of law specifically intended to inflict severe physical or mental pain or suffering (other than pain or suffering incidental to lawful sanctions) upon [a] person within his custody or physical control."	Seventeen thru Nineteen
International Covenant on Human Rights (ratified by U.S.)	Art. 7: "No one shall be subjected to torture or to cruel, inhuman or degrading treatment or punishment." Art. 10: "All persons deprived of their liberty shall be treated with humanity and with respect for the inherent dignity of the human person."	Seventeen thru Nineteen

ARTICLES OF IMPEACHMENT
FOR PRESIDENT GEORGE W. BUSH

U.S. AND INTERNATIONAL VIOLATIONS ALLEGED

INTRODUCED BY REP. DENNIS KUCINICH (D. Ohio)
JUNE 09, 2008 ·

Convention against Torture (ratified by U.S.)	Art. 2 (1) Each State Party shall take effective…measures to prevent acts of torture in …its jurisdiction. (2) No exceptional circumstances whatsoever, whether a state of war or a threat of war, internal political instability or any other public emergency, may be invoked as a justification of torture. (3) An order from a superior officer or a public authority may not be invoked as a justification of torture.	Seventeen thru Nineteen
Convention against Torture (ratified by U.S.)°	Art. 3. No State Party shall expel, return… or extradite a person to another State where there are substantial grounds for believing that he would be in danger of being subjected to torture	Nineteen
War Crimes Act of 1996 Title 18, U.S. Code, Section 2441	Makes it a crime for U.S. military personnel and nationals to commit war crimes as specified in the 1949 Geneva Conventions, including violations of Common Article 3 which prohibits: "violence to life and person, in particular murder of all kinds, mutilation, cruel treatment and torture; …outrages upon personal dignity, in particular humiliating and degrading treatment."	Seventeen thru Twenty
Optional Protocol to Fourth Geneva Convention on Rights of the Child (signed by U.S. in 2002)	Children under the age of 18 captured in conflicts are "protected persons" to be considered victims, not prisoners.	Twenty
Title 18, U.S. Code, Section 1385	Prohibits using military for domestic law enforcement without congressional authorization.	Twenty-three

ARTICLES OF IMPEACHMENT
FOR PRESIDENT GEORGE W. BUSH

U.S. AND INTERNATIONAL VIOLATIONS ALLEGED

INTRODUCED BY REP. DENNIS KUCINICH (D. Ohio)
JUNE 09, 2008

Foreign Intelligence Surveillance Act of 1978 ("FISA")	Provides that FISA is the exclusive means by which domestic electronic surveillance for foreign intelligence purposes can be conducted and criminalizes violations.	Twenty-four; Twenty-five
U.S. Constitution, Fourth Amendment	"The right of the people to be secure in their persons, houses, papers and effects, against unreasonable searches and seizures, shall not be violated, and no warrants shall issue, but upon probable cause, supported by oath...particularly describing the place to be searched, and the persons or things to be seized."	Twenty-four; Twenty-five
Voting Rights Act of 1965, Sec. 2	" No voting qualification or prerequisite to voting, or standard, practice, or procedure shall be imposed or applied by any State or political subdivision to deny or abridge the right of any citizen of the U. S. to vote on account of race or color. "	Twenty-eight; Twenty-nine
Title 2, U.S. Code, Sec. 194	Provides that when Congress certifies that a witness has failed to appear or produce records as required by subpoena, the "appropriate United States Attorney ...shall...bring the matter before the grand jury for its action."	Twenty-eight; Twenty-nine
Stored Communications Act of 1986	Prohibits knowing disclosure of customer telephone records to the government unless: (1) pursuant to subpoena, warrant or a National Security Letter (or other Administrative subpoena); with the customers lawful consent; (2) there is a business necessity; or (3) an emergency involving the danger of death or serious physical injury.	Article Twenty-five

ARTICLES OF IMPEACHMENT

Dennis J. Kucinich of Ohio
In the United States House of Representatives
Monday, June 9th, 2008

A Resolution
ARTICLES OF IMPEACHMENT
FOR PRESIDENT GEORGE W. BUSH

Resolved, that President George W. Bush be impeached for high crimes and misdemeanors, and that the following articles of impeachment be exhibited to the United States Senate:

Articles of impeachment exhibited by the House of Representatives of the United States of America in the name of itself and of the people of the United States of America, in maintenance and support of its impeachment against President George W. Bush for high crimes and misdemeanors.

In his conduct while President of the United States, George W. Bush, in violation of his constitutional oath to faithfully execute the office of President of the United States and, to the best of his ability, preserve, protect, and defend the Constitution of the United States, and in violation of his constitutional duty to take care that the laws be faithfully executed, has committed the following abuses of power.

Article I

CREATING A SECRET PROPAGANDA CAMPAIGN
TO MANUFACTURE A FALSE CASE
FOR WAR AGAINST IRAQ

In his conduct while President of the United States, George W. Bush, in violation of his constitutional oath to faithfully execute the office of President of the United States and, to the best of his ability, preserve, protect, and defend the Constitution of the United States, and in violation of his constitutional duty under Article II, Section 3 of the Constitution "to take care that the laws be faithfully executed," has both personally and acting through his agents and subordinates, together with the Vice President, illegally spent public dollars on a secret propaganda program to manufacture a false cause for war against Iraq.

The Department of Defense (DOD) has engaged in a years-long secret domestic propaganda campaign to promote the invasion and occupation of Iraq. This secret program was defended by the White House Press Secretary following its exposure. This program follows the pattern of crimes detailed in Article I, II, IV and VIII. The mission of this program placed it within the field controlled by the White House Iraq Group (WHIG), a White House task-force formed in August 2002 to market an invasion of Iraq to the American people. The group included Karl Rove, I. Lewis Libby, Condoleezza Rice, Karen Hughes, Mary Matalin, Stephen Hadley, Nicholas E. Calio, and James R. Wilkinson.

The WHIG produced white papers detailing so-called intelligence of Iraq's nuclear threat that later proved to be false. This supposed intelligence included the claim that Iraq had sought uranium from Niger as well as the claim that the high strength aluminum tubes Iraq purchased from China were to be used for the sole purpose of building centrifuges to enrich uranium. Unlike the National Intelligence Estimate of 2002, the WHIG's white papers provided "gripping images and stories" and used "literary license" with intelligence. The WHIG's white papers were written at the same time and by

3

the same people as speeches and talking points prepared for President Bush and some of his top officials.

The WHIG also organized a media blitz in which, between September 7-8, 2002, President Bush and his top advisers appeared on numerous interviews and all provided similarly gripping images about the possibility of nuclear attack by Iraq. The timing was no coincidence, as Andrew Card explained in an interview regarding waiting until after Labor Day to try to sell the American people on military action against Iraq, "From a marketing point of view, you don't introduce new products in August."

September 7-8, 2002:

NBC's *Meet the Press*: Vice President Cheney accused Saddam of moving aggressively to develop nuclear weapons over the past 14 months to add to his stockpile of chemical and biological arms.

CNN: Then-National Security Adviser Rice said, regarding the likelihood of Iraq obtaining a nuclear weapon, "We don't want the smoking gun to be a mushroom cloud."

CBS: President Bush declared that Saddam was "six months away from developing a weapon," and cited satellite photos of construction in Iraq where weapons inspectors once visited as evidence that Saddam was trying to develop nuclear arms.

The Pentagon military analyst propaganda program was revealed in an April 20, 2002, *New York Times* article. The program illegally involved "covert attempts to mold opinion through the undisclosed use of third parties." Secretary of Defense Donald Rumsfeld recruited 75 retired military officers and gave them talking points to deliver on Fox, CNN, ABC, NBC, CBS, and MSNBC, and according to the *New York Times* report, which has not been disputed by the Pentagon or the White House, "Participants were instructed not to quote their briefers directly or otherwise describe their contacts with the Pentagon."

According to the Pentagon's own internal documents, the military analysts were considered "message force multipliers" or "surrogates" who would deliver administration "themes and messages" to millions of Americans "in the form of their own opinions." In fact, they did deliver the themes and the messages but did not reveal that the Pentagon had provided them with their talking points. Robert S. Bevelacqua, a retired Green Beret and Fox News military analyst described this as follows: "It was them saying, 'We need to stick our hands up your back and move your mouth for you.'"

Congress has restricted annual appropriations bills since 1951 with this language: "No part of any appropriation contained in this or any other Act shall be used for publicity or propaganda purposes within the United States not heretofore authorized by the Congress."

A March 21, 2005, report by the Congressional Research Service states that "publicity or propaganda" is defined by the US Government Accountability Office (GAO) to mean either (1) self-aggrandizement by public officials, (2) purely partisan activity, or (3) "covert propaganda."

These concerns about "covert propaganda" were also the basis for the GAO's standard for determining when government-funded video news releases are illegal:

"The failure of an agency to identify itself as the source of a prepackaged news story misleads the viewing public by encouraging the viewing audience to believe that the broadcasting news organization developed the information. The prepackaged news stories are purposefully designed to be indistinguishable from news segments broadcast to the public. When the television viewing public does not know that the stories they watched on television news programs about the government were in fact prepared by the government, the stories are, in this sense, no longer purely factual -- the essential fact of attribution is missing."

The White House's own Office of Legal Council stated in a memorandum written in 2005 following the controversy over the Armstrong Williams scandal:

"Over the years, GAO has interpreted 'publicity or propaganda' restrictions to preclude use of appropriated funds for, among other things, so-called 'covert propaganda.' ... Consistent with that view, the OLC determined in 1988 that a statutory prohibition on using appropriated funds for 'publicity or propaganda' precluded undisclosed agency funding of advocacy by third-party groups. We stated that 'covert attempts to mold opinion through the undisclosed use of third parties' would run afoul of restrictions on using appropriated funds for 'propaganda.'"

Asked about the Pentagon's propaganda program at White House press briefing in April 2008, White House Press Secretary Dana Perino defended it, not by arguing that it was legal but by suggesting that it "should" be: "Look, I didn't know look, I think that you guys should take a step back and look at this look, DOD has made a decision, they've decided to stop this program. But I would say that one of the things that we try to do in the administration is get information out to a variety of people so that everybody else can call them and ask their opinion about something. And I don't think that that should be against the law. And I think that it's absolutely appropriate to provide information to people who are seeking it and are going to be providing their opinions on it. It doesn't necessarily mean that all of those military analysts ever agreed with the administration. I think you can go back and look and think that a lot of their analysis was pretty tough on the administration. That doesn't mean that we shouldn't talk to people."

In all of these actions and decisions, President George W. Bush has acted in a manner contrary to his trust as President and Commander in Chief, and subversive of constitutional government, to the prejudice of the cause of law and justice and to the manifest injury of the people of the United States. Wherefore, President George W. Bush, by such conduct, is guilty of an impeachable offense warranting removal from office.

Article I notes

David Barstow, "Behind TV Analysts: Pentagon's Hidden Hand, *New York Times*, April 20, 2008." http://www.nytimes.com/2008/04/20/washington/20generals.html?_r=3&hp=&adxnnl=1&oref=slogin&adxnnlx=1221408098-QqIkH4HvYRwNO/rezDvaZw

Center for Media and Democracy, "Pentagon Pundit Scandal Broke the Law."

http://www.prwatch.org/node/7261

Joshua Bolton, "Memorandum For Heads of Departments and Agencies: Use of Government Funds for Video News Releases, March 11, 2005." http://www.whitehouse.gov/omb/memoranda/fy2005/m05-10.pdf

Steven G. Bradbury, "Memorandum For The General Counsels of the Executive Branch, March 1, 2005. http://www.whitehouse.gov/omb/memoranda/fy2005/m05-10.pdf.

Carl Levin, Letter to Secretary of Defense Robert Gates, April 22, 2008. http://levin.senate.gov/newsroom/supporting/2008/SASC.Gates.042308.pdf

Congresswoman Rosa L. DeLauro's letter to major news outlets asking them to disclose Ethics Standards for Military Analysts, April 24, 2008. http://www.historycommons.org/context.jsp?item=a042808levindelauro&scale=0#a042808levindelauro

NBC *Meet the Press*, Interview with Dick Cheney, September 8, 2002. http://www.mtholyoke.edu/acad/intrel/bush/meet.htm

"Parts of the Message Machine: Excerpts from Documents," *New York Times,* April 19, 2008. http://www.nytimes.com/interactive/2008/04/19/us/20080419_GENERALS_DOCS.html

Rep. Paul Hodes, "Congressman Hodes Calls for Hearing on Bush Administration Manipulation of Iraq War News Analysts," April 24, 2008. http://hodes.house.gov/PRArticle.aspx?NewsID=1522

David Barstow, "Two Inquiries Set on Pentagon Publicity Effort," *New York Times*, May 24, 2008. http://www.nytimes.com/2008/05/24/washington/24generals.html

Article II

FALSELY, SYSTEMATICALLY, AND WITH CRIMINAL INTENT
CONFLATING THE ATTACKS OF SEPTEMBER 11, 2001
WITH MISREPRESENTATION OF IRAQ
AS AN IMMINENT SECURITY THREAT
AS PART OF A FRAUDULENT JUSTIFICATION
FOR A WAR OF AGGRESSION

In his conduct while President of the United States, George W. Bush, in violation of his constitutional oath to faithfully execute the office of President of the United States and, to the best of his ability, preserve, protect, and defend the Constitution of the United States, and in violation of his constitutional duty under Article II, Section 3 of the Constitution "to take care that the laws be faithfully executed," has both personally and acting through his agents and subordinates, together with the Vice President, executed a calculated and wide-ranging strategy to deceive the citizens and Congress of the United States into believing that there was and is a connection between Iraq and Saddam Hussein on the one hand, and the attacks of September 11, 2001 and al Qaeda, on the other hand, so as to falsely justify the use of the United States Armed Forces against the nation of Iraq in a manner that is damaging to the national security interests of the United States, as well as to fraudulently obtain and maintain congressional authorization and funding for the use of such military force against Iraq, thereby interfering with and obstructing Congress's lawful functions of overseeing foreign affairs and declaring war.

The means used to implement this deception were and continue to be, first, allowing, authorizing and sanctioning the manipulation of intelligence analysis by those under his direction and control, including the Vice President and the Vice President's agents, and second, personally making, or causing, authorizing and allowing to be made through highly-placed subordinates, including the President's Chief of Staff, the White House Press Secretary and

7

other White House spokespersons, the Secretaries of State and Defense, the National Security Advisor, and their deputies and spokespersons, false and fraudulent representations to the citizens of the United States and Congress regarding an alleged connection between Saddam Hussein and Iraq, on the one hand, and the September 11th attacks and al Qaeda, on the other hand, that were half-true, literally true but misleading, and/or made without a reasonable basis and with reckless indifference to their truth, as well as omitting to state facts necessary to present an accurate picture of the truth as follows:

(A) On or about September 12, 2001, former terrorism advisor Richard Clarke personally informed the President that neither Saddam Hussein nor Iraq was responsible for the September 11th attacks. On September 18, Clarke submitted to the President's National Security Adviser Condoleezza Rice a memo he had written in response to George W. Bush's specific request that stated: (1) the case for linking Hussein to the September 11th attacks was weak; (2) only anecdotal evidence linked Hussein to al Qaeda; (3) Osama Bin Laden resented the secularism of Saddam Hussein; and (4) there was no confirmed reporting of Saddam Hussein cooperating with Bin Laden on unconventional weapons.

(B) Ten days after the September 11th attacks the President received a President's Daily Briefing which indicated that the US intelligence community had no evidence linking Saddam Hussein to the September 11th attacks and that there was "scant credible evidence that Iraq had any significant collaborative ties with Al Qaeda."

(C) In Defense Intelligence Terrorism Summary No. 044-02, issued in February 2002, the United States Defense Intelligence Agency cast significant doubt on the possibility of a Saddam Hussein–Al Qaeda conspiracy: "Saddam's regime is intensely secular and is wary of Islamic revolutionary movements. Moreover, Baghdad is unlikely to provide assistance to a group it cannot control."

D) The October 2002 National Intelligence Estimate gave a "Low Confidence" rating to the notion of whether "in desperation Saddam would share chemical or biological weapons with Al Qaeda." The CIA never informed the President that there was an operational relationship between Al Qaeda and Saddam Hussein; on the contrary, its most "aggressive" analysis contained in "Iraq and al-Qaeda-Interpreting a Murky Relationship" dated June 21, 2002 "was that Iraq had had sporadic, wary contacts with al

Qaeda since the mid-1990s rather than a relationship with al Qaeda that has developed over time."

(E) Notwithstanding his knowledge that neither Saddam Hussein nor Iraq was in any way connected to the September 11th attacks, the President allowed and authorized those acting under his direction and control, including Vice President Richard B. Cheney and Lewis Libby, who reported directly to both the President and the Vice President, and Secretary of Defense Donald Rumsfeld, among others, to pressure intelligence analysts to alter their assessments and to create special units outside of, and unknown to, the intelligence community in order to secretly obtain unreliable information, to manufacture intelligence or reinterpret raw data in ways that would further the Bush administration's goal of fraudulently establishing a relationship not only between Iraq and al Qaeda, but between Iraq and the attacks of September 11th.

(F) Further, despite his full awareness that Iraq and Saddam Hussein had no relationship to the September 11th attacks, the President, and those acting under his direction and control have, since at least 2002 and continuing to the present, repeatedly issued public statements deliberately worded to mislead, words calculated in their implication to bring unrelated actors and circumstances into an artificially contrived reality thereby facilitating the systematic deception of Congress and the American people. Thus the public and some members of Congress, came to believe, falsely, that there was a connection between Iraq and the attacks of 9/11. This was accomplished through well-publicized statements by the Bush Administration which contrived to continually tie Iraq and 9/11 in the same statements of grave concern without making an explicit charge:

(1) "[If] Iraq regimes [sic] continues to defy us, and the world, we will move deliberately, yet decisively, to hold Iraq to account...It's a new world we're in. We used to think two oceans could separate us from an enemy. On that tragic day, September the 11th, 2001, we found out that's not the case. We found out this great land of liberty and of freedom and of justice is vulnerable. And therefore we must do everything we can—everything we can—to secure the homeland, to make us safe." Speech of President Bush in Iowa on September 16, 2002.

(2) "With every step the Iraqi regime takes toward gaining and deploying the most terrible weapons, our own options to confront that regime will narrow. And if an emboldened regime were to supply these weapons to

terrorist allies, then the attacks of September 11th would be a prelude to far greater horrors." —March 6, 2003, Statement of President Bush in National Press Conference.

(3) "The battle of Iraq is one victory in a war on terror that began on September the 11th, 2001—and still goes on. That terrible morning, 19 evil men—the shock troops of a hateful ideology—gave America and the civilized world a glimpse of their ambitions. They imagined, in the words of one terrorist, that September the 11th would be the 'beginning of the end of America.' By seeking to turn our cities into killing fields, terrorists and their allies believed that they could destroy this nation's resolve, and force our retreat from the world. They have failed." —May 1, 2003, Speech of President Bush on USS Abraham Lincoln.

(4) "Now we're in a new and unprecedented war against violent Islamic extremists. This is an ideological conflict we face against murderers and killers who try to impose their will. These are the people that attacked us on September the 11th and killed nearly 3,000 people. The stakes are high, and once again, we have had to change our strategic thinking. The major battleground in this war is Iraq." —June 28, 2007, Speech of President Bush at the Naval War College in Newport, Rhode Island.

(G) Notwithstanding his knowledge that there was no credible evidence of a working relationship between Saddam Hussein and Al Qaeda and that the intelligence community had specifically assessed that there was no such operational relationship, the President, both personally and through his subordinates and agents, has repeatedly falsely represented, both explicitly and implicitly, and through the misleading use of selectively-chosen facts, to the citizens of the United States and to the Congress that there was and is such an ongoing operational relationship, to wit:

(1) "We know that Iraq and al Qaeda have had high-level contacts that go back a decade. Some al Qaeda leaders who fled Afghanistan went to Iraq. These include one very senior al Qaeda leader who received medical treatment in Baghdad this year, and who has been associated with planning for chemical and biological attacks. We've learned that Iraq has trained al Qaeda members in bomb-making and poisons and deadly gases." —September 28, 2002, Weekly Radio Address of President Bush to the Nation.

(2) "[W]e we need to think about Saddam Hussein using al Qaeda to do his dirty work, to not leave fingerprints behind." —October 14, 2002, Remarks by President Bush in Michigan.

(3) "We know he's got ties with al Qaeda." —November 1, 2002, Speech of President Bush in New Hampshire.

(4) "Evidence from intelligence sources, secret communications, and statements by people now in custody reveal that Saddam Hussein aids and protects terrorists, including members of al Qaeda. Secretly, and without fingerprints, he could provide one of his hidden weapons to terrorists, or help them develop their own." —January 28, 2003, President Bush's State of the Union Address.

(5) "[W]hat I want to bring to your attention today is the potentially much more sinister nexus between Iraq and the al Qaeda terrorist network, a nexus that combines classic terrorist organizations and modern methods of murder. Iraq today harbors a deadly terrorist network..." —February 5, 2003, Speech of Former Secretary of State Colin Powell to the United Nations.

(6) "The battle of Iraq is one victory in a war on terror that began on September the 11, 2001 — and still goes on.... [T]he liberation of Iraq... removed an ally of al Qaeda." —May 1, 2003, Speech of President Bush on US S. Abraham Lincoln

(H) The Senate Select Committee on Intelligence Report on Whether Public Statements Regarding Iraq By US Government Officials Were Substantiated By Intelligence Information, which was released on June 5, 2008, concluded that:

(1) "Statements and implications by the President and Secretary of State suggesting that Iraq and al-Qa'ida had a partnership, or that Iraq had provided al-Qa'ida with weapons training, were not substantiated by the intelligence."

(2) "The Intelligence Community did not confirm that Muhammad Atta met an Iraqi intelligence officer in Prague in 2001 as the Vice President repeatedly claimed."

Through his participation and instance in the breathtaking scope of this deception, the President has used the highest office of trust to wage of campaign of deception of such sophistication as to deliberately subvert the national security interests of the United States. His dishonesty set the stage for the loss of more than 4000 United States service members; injuries to tens of thousands of soldiers, the loss of more than 1,000,000 innocent Iraqi citizens since the United States invasion; the loss of approximately $527 billion in war costs which has increased our Federal debt and the ultimate expenditure of three to five trillion dollars for all costs covering the war; the loss of military readiness within the United States Armed Services due to overextension, the lack of training and lack of equipment; the loss of United States credibility in world affairs; and the decades of likely blowback created by the invasion of Iraq.

In all of these actions and decisions, President George W. Bush has acted in a manner contrary to his trust as President and Commander in Chief, and subversive of constitutional government, to the prejudice of the cause of law and justice and to the manifest injury of the people of the United States. Wherefore, President George W. Bush, by such conduct, is guilty of an impeachable offense warranting removal from office.

Article II notes

Senate Select Committee on Intelligence, "Report on Whether Public Statements Regarding Iraq By US Government Officials Were Substantiated By Intelligence Information, June 5, 2008. http://intelligence.senate.gov/080605/phase2a.pdf

Iraq on the Record Report: "The Bush Administration's Public Statements on Iraq, by Minority Staff," March 16, 2004. http://oversight.house.gov/IraqOnTheRecord/pdf_admin_iraq_on_the_record_rep.pdf

Elizabeth de la Vega, "White House Criminal Conspiracy," The Nation, November 14, 2005. http://www.thenation.com/doc/20051114/delavega .

Richard Clarke, Against All Enemies, New York, Free Press, 2004.

National Commission on Terrorist Attacks Upon the United States, Report, Section 10.3, September 20, 2004. http://www.9-11commission.gov/report/911Report_Ch10.htm

Waas, Murray, "Key Bush Intelligence Briefing Kept From Hill Panel," National Journal 22 November 2005.

Jehl, Douglas, "Report Warned Bush Team About Intelligence Doubts," New York Times, November 6, 2005.

"Declassified Key Judgments from National Intelligence Estimate," October 2002. http://www.fas.org/irp/cia/product/iraq-wmd.html

Report of the Senate Select Committee on Intelligence, (305-307. 321-323), July 9, 2004. http://intelligence.senate.gov/prewar.pdf

Office of the Inspector General's Review of the Pre-Iraqi War Activities of the Office of the Undersecretary of Defense for Policy, Executive Summary, February 9, 2007. http://levin.senate.gov/newsroom/supporting/2007/SASC.DODIGFeithreport.040507.pdf

Pincus, Walter and Priest, Dana. "Some Iraq Analysts Felt Pressure From Cheney Visits." Washington Post, June 5, 2003: A01.

Hersh, Seymour M. "The Stovepipe." The New Yorker, October 27, 2003.

Speech of President Bush in Davenport, Iowa, September 16, 2002. http://www.whitehouse.gov/news/releases/2002/09/20020916-2.html

Article II

Remarks of President Bush in National Press Conference, March 6, 2003. http://www.whitehouse.gov/news/releases/2003/03/20030306-8.html

Speech of President Bush aboard USS. Abraham Lincoln, May 1, 2003. http://www.whitehouse.gov/news/releases/2003/05/20030501-15.html

Speech of President Bush at Naval War College in Newport, Rhode Island, June, 28, 2007. http://www.whitehouse.gov/news/releases/2007/06/20070628-14.html

Iraq on the Record Report: Bush Administration's Public Statements on Iraq, by Minority Staff; Iraq-al Qaeda connection; March 16, 2004. http://oversight.house.gov/IraqOnTheRecord/index.asp?viewAll=1&Subject=Al%2DQaeda&submit=display

Radio Address by President Bush to the Nation, September 28, 2002. http://www.whitehouse.gov/news/releases/2002/09/20020928.html

Remarks by President Bush in Waterford, Michigan, October 14, 2002. http://www.whitehouse.gov/news/releases/2002/10/20021014-4.html

Remarks by President Bush in Portsmouth, New Hampshire, November 1, 2002. http://www.whitehouse.gov/news/releases/2002/11/20021101-5.html

President Bush Delivers State of the Union Address, January 28, 2003. http://www.whitehouse.gov/news/releases/2003/01/20030128-19.html

Secretary of State Colin Powell Addresses UN Security Council, February 5, 2003. http://www.whitehouse.gov/news/releases/2003/02/20030205-1.html

Speech of President Bush aboard USS. Abraham Lincoln, May 1, 2003. http://www.whitehouse.gov/news/releases/2003/05/20030501-15.html

Operation Iraqi Freedom (OIF) Casualty Status, Department of Defense. http://kucinich.house.gov/UploadedFiles/clo1.pdf

Gilbert Burnham, et al, "Mortality After the 2003 Invasion of Iraq, The Lancet, October 11, 2006. http://kucinich.house.gov/UploadedFiles/clo2.pdf

Amy Belasco, "The Cost of Iraq, Afghanistan and Other Global War on Terror Operations Since 9/11," Congressional Research Service, March 14, 2007. http://kucinich.house.gov/UploadedFiles/clo3.pdf

Lawrence Korb, "A troop readiness crisis," Boston Globe, April 11, 2007. http://kucinich.house.gov/UploadedFiles/clo4.pdf

Article III

MISLEADING THE AMERICAN PEOPLE AND MEMBERS OF CONGRESS TO BELIEVE IRAQ POSSESSED WEAPONS OF MASS DESTRUCTION, SO AS TO MANUFACTURE A FALSE CASE FOR WAR

In his conduct while President of the United States, George W. Bush, in violation of his constitutional oath to faithfully execute the office of President of the United States and, to the best of his ability, preserve, protect, and defend the Constitution of the United States, and in violation of his constitutional duty under Article II, Section 3 of the Constitution "to take care that the laws be faithfully executed," has both personally and acting through his agents and subordinates, together with the Vice President, executed instead a calculated and wide-ranging strategy to deceive the citizens and Congress of the United States into believing that the nation of Iraq possessed weapons of mass destruction in order to justify the use of the United States Armed Forces against the nation of Iraq in a manner damaging to our national security interests, thereby interfering with and obstructing Congress's lawful functions of overseeing foreign affairs and declaring war.

The means used to implement this deception were and continue to be personally making, or causing, authorizing and allowing to be made through highly-placed subordinates, including the President's Chief of Staff, the White House Press Secretary and other White House spokespersons, the Secretaries of State and Defense, the National Security Advisor, and their deputies and spokespersons, false and fraudulent representations to the citizens of the United States and Congress regarding Iraq's alleged possession of biological, chemical and nuclear weapons that were half-true, literally true but misleading, and/or made without a reasonable basis and with reckless indifference to their truth, as well as omitting to state facts necessary to present an accurate picture of the truth as follows:

(A) Long before the March 19, 2003 invasion of Iraq, a wealth of intelligence informed the President and those under his direction and control that Iraq's stockpiles of chemical and biological weapons had been destroyed well before 1998 and that there was little, if any, credible intelligence that showed otherwise. As reported in the Washington Post in March of 2003, in 1995, Saddam Hussein's son-in-law Hussein Kamel had informed US and British intelligence officers that "all weapons—biological, chemical, missile, nuclear were destroyed." In September 2002, the Defense Intelligence Agency issued a report that concluded: "A substantial amount of Iraq's chemical warfare agents, precursors, munitions and production equipment were destroyed between 1991 and 1998 as a result of Operation Desert Storm and UNSCOM actions...[T]here is no reliable information on whether Iraq is producing and stockpiling chemical weapons or whether Iraq has-or will-establish its chemical warfare agent production facilities." Notwithstanding the absence of evidence proving that such stockpiles existed and in direct contradiction to substantial evidence that showed they did not exist, the President and his subordinates and agents made numerous false representations claiming with certainty that Iraq possessed chemical and biological weapons that it was developing to use to attack the United States, to wit:

(1) "[T]he notion of a Saddam Hussein with his great oil wealth, with his inventory that he already has of biological and chemical weapons... is, I think, a frightening proposition for anybody who thinks about it." —Statement of Vice President Cheney on CBS's *Face the Nation*, March 24, 2002.

(2) "In defiance of the United Nations, Iraq has stockpiled biological and chemical weapons, and is rebuilding the facilities used to make more of those weapons." —Speech of President Bush, October 5, 2002.

(3) "All the world has now seen the footage of an Iraqi Mirage aircraft with a fuel tank modified to spray biological agents over wide areas. Iraq has developed spray devices that could be used on unmanned aerial vehicles with ranges far beyond what is permitted by the Security Council. A UAV launched from a vessel off the American coast could reach hundreds of miles inland." —Statement by President Bush from the White House, February 6, 2003.

(B) Despite overwhelming intelligence in the form of statements and reports filed by and on behalf of the CIA, the State Department and the IAEA, among others, which indicated that the claim was untrue, the President, and those under his direction and control, made numerous representations claiming and implying through misleading language that Iraq was attempting to purchase uranium from Niger in order to falsely buttress its argument that Iraq was reconstituting its nuclear weapons program, including:

(1) "The regime has the scientists and facilities to build nuclear weapons, and is seeking the materials needed to do so." —Statement of President Bush from White House, October 2, 2002.

(2) "The [Iraqi] report also failed to deal with issues which have arisen since 1998, including: . . attempts to acquire uranium and the means to enrich it." —Letter from President Bush to Vice President Cheney and the Senate, January 20, 2003.

(3) "The British Government has learned that Saddam Hussein recently sought significant quantities of uranium from Africa." —President Bush Delivers State of the Union Address, January 28, 2003.

(C) Despite overwhelming evidence in the form of reports by nuclear weapons experts from the Energy, the Defense and State Departments, as well from outside and international agencies which assessed that aluminum tubes the Iraqis were purchasing were not suitable for nuclear centrifuge use and were, on the contrary, identical to ones used in rockets already being manufactured by the Iraqis, the President, and those under his direction and control, persisted in making numerous false and fraudulent representations implying and stating explicitly that the Iraqis were purchasing the tubes for use in a nuclear weapons program, to wit:

(1) "We do know that there have been shipments going . . . into Iraq...of aluminum tubes that really are only suited to—high-quality aluminum tools [sic] that are only really suited for nuclear weapons programs, centrifuge programs." —Statement of then-National Security Advisor Condoleezza Rice on CNN's Late Edition with Wolf Blitzer, September 8, 2002.

(2) "Our intelligence sources tell us that he has attempted to purchase high-strength aluminum tubes suitable for nuclear weapons production." —President Bush's State of the Union Address, January 28, 2003.

(3) "[H]e has made repeated covert attempts to acquire high-specification aluminum tubes from 11 different countries, even after inspections resumed.... By now, just about everyone has heard of these tubes and we all know that there are differences of opinion. There is controversy about what these tubes are for. Most US experts think they are intended to serve as

rotors in centrifuges used to enrich uranium." —Speech of Former Secretary of State Colin Powell to the United Nations, February 5, 2003.

(D) The President, both personally and acting through those under his direction and control, suppressed material information, selectively declassified information for the improper purposes of retaliating against a whistleblower and presenting a misleading picture of the alleged threat from Iraq, facilitated the exposure of the identity of a covert CIA operative and thereafter not only failed to investigate the improper leaks of classified information from within his administration, but also failed to cooperate with an investigation into possible federal violations resulting from this activity and, finally, entirely undermined the prosecution by commuting the sentence of Lewis Libby citing false and insubstantial grounds, all in an effort to prevent Congress and the citizens of the United States from discovering the fraudulent nature of the President's claimed justifications for the invasion of Iraq.

(E) The Senate Select Committee on Intelligence Report on Whether Public Statements Regarding Iraq By US Government Officials Were Substantiated By Intelligence Information, which was released on June 5, 2008, concluded that:

(1) "Statements by the President and Vice President prior to the October 2002 National Intelligence Estimate regarding Iraq's chemical weapons production capability and activities did not reflect the intelligence community's uncertainties as to whether such production was ongoing."

(2) "The Secretary of Defense's statement that the Iraqi government operated underground WMD facilities that were not vulnerable to conventional airstrikes because they were underground and deeply buried was not substantiated by available intelligence information."

(3) Chairman of the Senate Intelligence Committee Jay Rockefeller concluded: "In making the case for war, the Administration repeatedly presented intelligence as fact when in reality it was unsubstantiated, contradicted, or even non-existent. As a result, the American people were led to believe that the threat from Iraq was much greater than actually existed."

The President has subverted the national security interests of the United States by setting the stage for the loss of more than 4000 United States service members and the injury to tens of thousands of US soldiers; the loss of more than 1,000,000 innocent Iraqi citizens since the United States invasion; the loss of approximately $500 billion in war costs which has increased our Federal debt with a long term financial cost of between three and five trillion dollars; the loss of military readiness within the United States Armed Services due to overextension, the lack of training and lack of equipment; the loss of United States credibility in world affairs; and the decades of likely blowback created by the invasion of Iraq.

In all of these actions and decisions, President George W. Bush has acted in a manner contrary to his trust as President and Commander in Chief, and subversive of constitutional government, to the prejudice of the cause of law and justice and to the manifest injury of the people of the United States. Wherefore, President George W. Bush, by such conduct, is guilty of an impeachable offense warranting removal from office.

Article III notes

Senate Select Committee on Intelligence, "Report on Whether Public Statements Regarding Iraq By US Government Officials Were Substantiated By Intelligence Information," June 5, 2008. http://intelligence.senate.gov/080605/phase2a.pdf

Iraq on the Record, "Bush Administration's Public Statements about Chemical and Biological Weapons," March 16, 2004.

http://oversight.house.gov/IraqOnTheRecord/index.asp?viewAll=1&Subject=Chemical+and+Biological+Weapons&submit=display

Dana Milbank and Walter Pincus, "President Clings to Dubious Allegations about Iraq," *The Washington Post*, March 17, 2003. http://www.washingtonpost.com/ac2/wp-dyn/A42517-2003-Mar17?language=printer

Statement of Vice President Cheney on *Face the Nation*, March 24, 2002. http://www.whitehouse.gov/vicepresident/newsspeeches/speeches/vp20020324-1.html

Radio Address of President Bush to the Nation, October 5, 2002. http://www.whitehouse.gov/news/releases/2002/10/20021005.html

Statement by President Bush from the White House, February 6, 2003. http://www.whitehouse.gov/news/releases/2003/02/20030206-17.html

Congressman John Conyers, "George W. Bush versus the US Constitution," 2006. http://www.afterdowningstreet.org/constitutionincrisis

Statement of President Bush from White House, October 2, 2002. http://www.whitehouse.gov/news/releases/2003/01/20030128-19.html

President Bush's State of the Union Address, January 28, 2003. http://www.whitehouse.gov/news/releases/2003/01/20030128-19.html

Iraq on the Record Report, "The Bush Administration's Public Statements on Iraq," by Minority Staff, March 16, 2004, 10-13. http://oversight.house.gov/IraqOnTheRecord/pdf_admin_iraq_on_the_record_rep.pdf .

Article III

Statement of then National Security Advisor Condoleezza Rice on CNN's *Late Edition* with Wolf Blitzer, September 8, 2003. http://archives.cnn.com/2002/ALLPOLITICS/09/08/iraq.debate/

President Bush Delivers State of the Union Address, January 28, 2003. http://www.whitehouse.gov/news/releases/2003/01/20030128-19.html

Secretary of State Colin Powell Addresses UN Security Council, February 5, 2003. http://www.whitehouse.gov/news/releases/2003/02/20030205-1.html

Murray Waas, "Bush Directed Cheney To Counter War Critic, *National Journal*, July 3, 2006. http://news.nationaljournal.com/articles/0703nj1.htm

Elizabeth de la Vega, "Final Jeopardy," TomDispatch.com, April 9, 2006. http://www.tomdispatch.com/post/76008/de_la_vega_on_the_president_s_final_jeopardy_question

Letter from Representative Henry Waxman to then White House Chief of Staff Andrew Card, July 14, 2005. http://oversight.house.gov/documents/20050714122956-30175.pdf

Letter from Representative Henry Waxman to White House Chief of Staff Joshua Bolten, March 16, 2007. http://oversight.house.gov/documents/20070316154127-11403.pdf

Letter from Representative Henry Waxman to Attorney General Michael Mukasey, December 3, 2007. http://oversight.house.gov/documents/20071203103022.pdf

Jon Ponder, "Did Bush Lie to Federal Investigators in the CIA Leak Case?" *Pensito Review,* November 21, 2007. http://www.pensitoreview.com/2007/11/21/did-bush-lie-to-fitzgerald-too1

Gilbert Burnham, et al, "Mortality After the 2003 Invasion of Iraq," October 11, 2006, *The Lancet.* http://kucinich.house.gov/UploadedFiles/clo2.pdf .

Amy Belasco, "The Cost of Iraq, Afghanistan and Other Global War on Terror Operations Since 9/11," Congressional Research Service, March 14, 2007. http://kucinich.house.gov/UploadedFiles/clo3.pdf

Lawrence Korb, "A Troop Readiness Crisis," *Boston Globe*, April 11, 2007. http://kucinich.house.gov/UploadedFiles/clo4.pdf

Article IV

MISLEADING THE AMERICAN PEOPLE AND MEMBERS OF CONGRESS TO BELIEVE IRAQ POSED AN IMMINENT THREAT TO THE UNITED STATES

In his conduct while President of the United States, George W. Bush, in violation of his constitutional oath to faithfully execute the office of President of the United States and, to the best of his ability, preserve, protect, and defend the Constitution of the United States, and in violation of his constitutional duty under Article II, Section 3 of the Constitution "to take care that the laws be faithfully executed," has both personally and acting through his agents and subordinates, together with the Vice President, executed a calculated and wide-ranging strategy to deceive the citizens and Congress of the United States into believing that the nation of Iraq posed an imminent threat to the United States in order to justify the use of the United States Armed Forces against the nation of Iraq in a manner damaging to our national security interests, thereby interfering with and obstructing Congress's lawful functions of overseeing foreign affairs and declaring war.

The means used to implement this deception were and continue to be, first, allowing, authorizing and sanctioning the manipulation of intelligence analysis by those under his direction and control, including the Vice President and the Vice President's agents, and second, personally making, or causing, authorizing and allowing to be made through highly-placed subordinates, including the President's Chief of Staff, the White House Press Secretary and other White House spokespersons, the Secretaries of State and Defense, the National Security Advisor, and their deputies and spokespersons, false and fraudulent representations to the citizens of the United States and Congress regarding an alleged urgent threat posed by Iraq, statements that were half-true, literally true but misleading, and/or made without a reasonable basis and with reckless indifference to their truth, as well as omitting to state facts necessary to present an accurate picture of the truth as follows:

20

(A) Notwithstanding the complete absence of intelligence analysis to support a claim that Iraq posed an imminent or urgent threat to the United States and the intelligence community's assessment that Iraq was in fact not likely to attack the United States unless it was itself attacked, President Bush, both personally and through his agents and subordinates, made, allowed and caused to be made repeated false representations to the citizens and Congress of the United States implying and explicitly stating that such a dire threat existed, including the following:

(1) "States such as these [Iraq, Iran and North Korea] and their terrorist allies constitute an axis of evil, arming to threaten the peace of the world. By seeking weapons of mass destruction, these regimes pose a grave and growing danger. They could provide these arms to terrorists, giving them the means to match their hatred. They could attack our allies or attempt to blackmail the United States. In any of these cases, the price of indifference would be catastrophic." —President Bush's State of the Union Address, January 29, 2002.

(2) "Simply stated, there is no doubt that Saddam Hussein has weapons of mass destruction. He is amassing them to use against our friends our enemies and against us." —Speech of Vice President Cheney at VFW 103rd National Convention, August 26, 2002.

(3) "The history, the logic, and the facts lead to one conclusion: Saddam Hussein's regime is a grave and gathering danger. To suggest otherwise is to hope against the evidence. To assume this regime's good faith is to bet the lives of millions and the peace of the world in a reckless gamble. And this is a risk we must not take." —Address of President Bush to the United Nations General Assembly, September 12, 2002.

(4) "[N]o terrorist state poses a greater or more immediate threat to the security of our people than the regime of Saddam Hussein and Iraq." —Statement of Former Defense Secretary Donald Rumsfeld to Congress, September 19, 2002.

(5) "On its present course, the Iraqi regime is a threat of unique urgency. . . . it has developed weapons of mass death." —Statement of President Bush at White House, October 2, 2002.

(6) "But the President also believes that this problem has to be dealt with, and if the United Nations won't deal with it, then the United States, with other likeminded nations, may have to deal with it. We would prefer not to go that route, but the danger is so great, with respect to Saddam

Hussein having weapons of mass destruction, and perhaps even terrorists getting hold of such weapons, that it is time for the international community to act, and if it doesn't act, the President is prepared to act with likeminded nations." —Statement of Former Secretary of State Colin Powell in interview with Ellen Ratner of *Talk Radio News*, October 30, 2002.

(7) "Today the world is also uniting to answer the unique and urgent threat posed by Iraq. A dictator who has used weapons of mass destruction on his own people must not be allowed to produce or possess those weapons. We will not permit Saddam Hussein to blackmail and/or terrorize nations which love freedom." —Speech by President Bush to Prague Atlantic Student Summit, November 20, 2002.

(8) "But the risk of doing nothing, the risk of the security of this country being jeopardized at the hands of a madman with weapons of mass destruction far exceeds the risk of any action we may be forced to take." —President Bush Meets with National Economic Council at White House, February 25, 2003.

(B) In furtherance of his fraudulent effort to deceive Congress and the citizens of the United States into believing that Iraq and Saddam Hussein posed an imminent threat to the United States, the President allowed and authorized those acting under his direction and control, including Vice President Richard B. Cheney, former Secretary of Defense Donald Rumsfeld, and Lewis Libby, who reportedly directly to both the President and the Vice President, among others, to pressure intelligence analysts to tailor their assessments and to create special units outside of, and unknown to, the intelligence community in order to secretly obtain unreliable information, to manufacture intelligence, or to reinterpret raw data in ways that would support the Bush administration's plan to invade Iraq based on a false claim of urgency despite the lack of justification for such a preemptive action.

(C) The Senate Select Committee on Intelligence Report on Whether Public Statements Regarding Iraq By US Government Officials Were Substantiated By Intelligence Information, which was released on June 5, 2008, concluded that:

(1) "Statements by the President and the Vice President indicating that Saddam Hussein was prepared to give weapons of mass destruction to terrorist groups for attacks against the United States were contradicted by available intelligence information."

Thus the President willfully and falsely misrepresented Iraq as an urgent threat requiring immediate action thereby subverting the national security interests of the United States by setting the stage for the loss of more than 4000 United States service members; the injuries to tens of thousands of US soldiers; the deaths of more than 1,000,000 Iraqi citizens since the United States invasion; the loss of approximately $527 billion in war costs which has increased our Federal debt and the ultimate costs of the war between three trillion and five trillion dollars; the loss of military readiness within the United States Armed Services due to overextension, the lack of training and lack of equipment; the loss of United States credibility in world affairs; and the decades of likely blowback created by the invasion of Iraq.

In all of these actions and decisions, President George W. Bush has acted in a manner contrary to his trust as President and Commander in Chief, and subversive of constitutional government, to the prejudice of the cause of law and justice and to the manifest injury of the people of the United States. Wherefore, President George W. Bush, by such conduct, is guilty of an impeachable offense warranting removal from office.

Article IV notes

Senate Select Committee on Intelligence, "Report on Whether Public Statements Regarding Iraq By US Government Officials Were Substantiated By Intelligence Information," June 5, 2008. http://intelligence.senate.gov/080605/phase2a.pdf

John Judis, "The Selling of the Iraq War, The First Casualty," New Republic, June 30, 2003. http://www.globalpolicy.org/security/issues/iraq/unmovic/2003/0630selling.htm

John Conyers, Constitution in Crisis, Chapter Two, Chronology, 2005. http://www.afterdowningstreet.org/downloads/section2.pdf

Remarks as Prepared for Delivery by Former CIA Director George J. Tenet at Georgetown University, February 5, 2004. http://www.fas.org/irp/cia/product/dci020504.html

Letter from Former CIA Director George Tenet to Senate Intelligence Committee, October 7, 2002. http://www.globalsecurity.org/wmd/library/news/iraq/2002/iraq-021007-cia01.htm

President Bush's State of the Union Address, January 29, 2002. http://www.whitehouse.gov/news/releases/2002/01/20020129-11.html

Speech of Vice President Cheney at VFW 103rd National Convention, August 26, 2002. http://www.whitehouse.gov/news/releases/2002/08/20020826.html

Address of President Bush to the United Nations General Assembly, September 12, 2002. http://www.whitehouse.gov/news/releases/2002/09/20020912-1.html

Testimony of Former Secretary of Defense Donald Rumsfeld to Senate Armed Services Committee, September 19, 2002. http://www.defenselink.mil/speeches/speech.aspx?speechid=287

The 35 Articles of Impeachment

Statement of President Bush at White House, October 2, 2002. http://www.whitehouse.gov/news/releases/2002/10/20021002-7.html

Statement of Former Secretary of State Colin Powell in Interview with Ellen Ratner, Talk Radio News, October 30, 2002. http://www.state.gov/secretary/former/powell/remarks/2002/14807.htm

Speech of President Bush to Prague Atlantic Student Summit, November 20, 2002. http://www.whitehouse.gov/news/releases/2002/11/20021120-4.html

Remarks of President Bush to National Economic Council at White House, February 25, 2003. http://www.whitehouse.gov/news/releases/2003/02/images/20030225-6_econ-022403-d-ed-1-515h.html

John Conyers, Constitution in Crisis, Chapter 3, 2005. http://www.afterdowningstreet.org/downloads/section3b.pdf

Gilbert Burnham, et al, "Mortality After the 2003 Invasion of Iraq," The Lancet, October 11, 2006. http://kucinich.house.gov/UploadedFiles/clo2.pdf

Amy Belasco, "The Cost of Iraq, Afghanistan and Other Global War on Terror Operations Since 9/11," Congressional Research Service, March 14, 2007. http://kucinich.house.gov/UploadedFiles/clo3.pdf

Lawrence Korb, "A Troop Readiness Crisis, Boston Globe, April 11, 2007. http://kucinich.house.gov/UploadedFiles/clo4.pdf

Article V

ILLEGALLY MISSPENDING FUNDS
TO SECRETLY BEGIN A WAR OF AGGRESSION

In his conduct while President of the United States, George W. Bush, in violation of his constitutional oath to faithfully execute the office of President of the United States and, to the best of his ability, preserve, protect, and defend the Constitution of the United States, and in violation of his constitutional duty under Article II, Section 3 of the Constitution "to take care that the laws be faithfully executed," has both personally and acting through his agents and subordinates, together with the Vice President, illegally misspent funds to begin a war in secret prior to any Congressional authorization.

The president used over $2 billion in the summer of 2002 to prepare for the invasion of Iraq. First reported in Bob Woodward's book, *Plan of Attack*, and later confirmed by the Congressional Research Service, Bush took money appropriated by Congress for Afghanistan and other programs and—with no Congressional notification -- used it to build airfields in Qatar and to make other preparations for the invasion of Iraq. This constituted a violation of Article I, Section 9 of the US Constitution, as well as a violation of the War Powers Act of 1973.

In all of these actions and decisions, President George W. Bush has acted in a manner contrary to his trust as President and Commander in Chief, and subversive of constitutional government, to the prejudice of the cause of law and justice and to the manifest injury of the people of the United States. Wherefore, President George W. Bush, by such conduct, is guilty of an impeachable offense warranting removal from office.

Article V notes

US Constitution. Article I, Section 9. http://www.house.gov/house/Constitution/Constitution.html

The War Powers Clause of the US Constitution

Congressman John Conyers, *The Constitution in Crisis: Misuse of Government Funds.*

(31 USC. § 1301)

Federal law makes it illegal to use government funds appropriated to the government for any purpose other than those specifically permitted by the appropriations. It specifically states that "appropriations shall be applied only to the objects for which the appropriations were made except as otherwise provided by law."

The illegal use of funds would cause an automatic diminution in funds available to the guilty agency. To determine whether a government activity is legal, it is important to understand whether the agency or office that engaged in the activity was permitted to expend funds for that specific purpose. See US GENERAL ACCOUNTING OFFICE, PRINCIPLES OF FEDERAL APPROPRIATIONS LAW 4-9 (3rd ed. 2004). As a general rule, of course, none of the functions of government offices include the dissemination of false information, the dissemination of information for political ends, or retribution against political opponents. For example, the Constitution provides that the President shall be commander-in-chief of the Armed Forces, have the authority to grant pardons, have the power to sign treaties, and nominate civil officers and ambassadors and judges. US CONST. art. II, s 2. Congress has provided funds to the President to hire staff and carry out his responsibilities; none of these appropriated funds is conditioned upon the President misleading the public or manipulating government agencies. See Pub. L. No. 108-7, Division J, title III (appropriations for fiscal year 2003 enacted in early 2003).

Article VI

INVADING IRAQ IN VIOLATION OF THE
REQUIREMENTS OF HJRes114

In his conduct while President of the United States, George W. Bush, in violation of his constitutional oath to faithfully execute the office of President of the United States and, to the best of his ability, preserve, protect, and defend the Constitution of the United States, and in violation of his constitutional duty under Article II, Section 3 of the Constitution "to take care that the laws be faithfully executed," exceeded his Constitutional authority to wage war by invading Iraq in 2003 without meeting the requirements of HJRes 114, the "Authorization for Use of Military Force Against Iraq Resolution of 2002," to wit:

(1) HJRes 114 contains several Whereas clauses consistent with statements being made by the White House at the time regarding the threat from Iraq as evidenced by the following:

(A) HJRes 114 states "Whereas Iraq both poses a continuing threat to the national security of the United States and international peace and security in the Persian Gulf region and remains in material and unacceptable breach of its international obligations by, among other things, continuing to possess and develop a significant chemical and biological weapons capability, actively seeking a nuclear weapons capability, and supporting and harboring terrorist organizations"; and

(B) HJRes 114 states "Whereas members of Al Qaeda, an organization bearing responsibility for attacks on the United States, its citizens, and interests, including the attacks that occurred on September 11, 2001, are known to be in Iraq."

(2) HJRes 114 states that the President must provide a determination, the truthfulness of which is implied, that military force is necessary in order to use the authorization, as evidenced by the following:

(A) Section 3 of HJRes 114 states:

27

"(B) PRESIDENTIAL DETERMINATION.—In connection with the exercise of the authority granted in subsection (a) to use force the President shall, prior to such exercise or as soon thereafter as may be feasible, but no later than 48 hours after exercising such authority, make available to the Speaker of the House of Representatives and the President pro tempore of the Senate his determination that—

(1) reliance by the United States on further diplomatic or other peaceful means alone either (A) will not adequately protect the national security of the United States against the continuing threat posed by Iraq or (B) is not likely to lead to enforcement of all relevant United Nations Security Council resolutions regarding Iraq; and

(2) acting pursuant to this joint resolution is consistent with the United States and other countries continuing to take the necessary actions against international terrorist and terrorist organizations, including those nations, organizations, or persons who planned, authorized, committed or aided the terrorist attacks that occurred on September 11, 2001."

(3) On March 18, 2003, President George Bush sent a letter to Congress stating that he had made that determination as evidenced by the following:

(A) March 18th, 2003 Letter to Congress stating:

"Consistent with section 3(b) of the Authorization for Use of Military Force Against Iraq Resolution of 2002 (Public Law 107-243), and based on information available to me, including that in the enclosed document, I determine that:

(1) reliance by the United States on further diplomatic and other peaceful means alone will neither (A) adequately protect the national security of the United States against the continuing threat posed by Iraq nor (B) likely lead to enforcement of all relevant United Nations Security Council resolutions regarding Iraq; and

(2) acting pursuant to the Constitution and Public Law 107-243 is consistent with the United States and other countries continuing to take the necessary actions against international terrorists and terrorist organizations, including those nations, organizations, or persons who planned, authorized, committed, or aided the terrorist attacks that occurred on September 11, 2001."

(4) President George Bush knew that these statements were false as evidenced by:

(A) Information provided with Article I, II, III, IV and V.

(B) A statement by President George Bush in an interview with Tony Blair on January 31st 2003: [WH]

Reporter: "One question for you both. Do you believe that there is a link between Saddam Hussein, a direct link, and the men who attacked on September the 11th?"

President Bush: "I can't make that claim."

(C) An article on February 19th by Terrorism expert Rohan Gunaratna states "I could find no evidence of links between Iraq and Al Qaeda. The documentation and interviews indicated that Al Qaeda regarded Saddam, a secular leader, as an infidel." *[International Herald Tribune]*

(D) According to a February 2nd, 2003 article in the *New York Times*:

At the Federal Bureau of Investigation, some investigators said they were baffled by the Bush administration's insistence on a solid link between Iraq and Osama bin Laden's network. "We've been looking at this hard for more than a year and you know what, we just don't think it's there," a government official said.

(5) Section 3C of HJRes 114 states that "Nothing in this joint resolution supersedes any requirement of the War Powers Resolution."

(6) The War Powers Resolution Section 9(d)(1) states:

(d) Nothing in this joint resolution—

(1) is intended to alter the constitutional authority of the Congress or of the President, or the provision of existing treaties; or

(7) The United Nations Charter was an existing treaty and, as shown in Article VIII, the invasion of Iraq violated that treaty.

(8) President George Bush knowingly failed to meet the requirements of HJRes 114 and violated the requirement of the War Powers Resolution and, thereby, invaded Iraq without the authority of Congress.

In all of these actions and decisions, President George W. Bush has acted in a manner contrary to his trust as President and Commander in Chief, and subversive of constitutional government, to the prejudice of the cause of law and justice and to the manifest injury of the people of the United States. Wherefore, President George W. Bush, by such conduct, is guilty of an impeachable offense warranting removal from office.

Article VI notes

White House statement, March 18, 2003. http://www.whitehouse.gov/news
releases/2003/03/20030319-1.html

White House report to Congress, March 18, 2003. http://afterdowningstreet.org/downloads/3-18-03report.pdf

President George W. Bush statement, January 31, 2003. http://www.whitehouse.gov/news/
releases/2003/01/20030131-23.html

Rohan Gunaratna, "Iraq and Al Qaeda, No Evidence of Alliance, International Herald Tribune. February 19, 2003. http://www.globalpolicy.org/security/issues/iraq/attack/2003/0219alliance.htm

James Risen and David Johnston, "Split at CIA and FBI on Iraqi Ties to Al Qaeda," New York Times, February 2, 2003. http://www.globalpolicy.org/security/issues/iraq/attack/2003/0202splitat.htm

War Powers Resolution. http://www.yale.edu/lawweb/avalon/warpower.htm

Article VII

INVADING IRAQ ABSENT A DECLARATION OF WAR

In his conduct while President of the United States, George W. Bush, in violation of his constitutional oath to faithfully execute the office of President of the United States and, to the best of his ability, preserve, protect, and defend the Constitution of the United States, and in violation of his constitutional duty under Article II, Section 3 of the Constitution "to take care that the laws be faithfully executed," has launched a war against Iraq absent any congressional declaration of war or equivalent action.

Article I, Section 8, Clause 11 (the War Powers Clause) makes clear that the United States Congress holds the exclusive power to decide whether or not to send the nation into war. "The Congress," the War Powers Clause states, "shall have power...To declare war..."

The October 2002 congressional resolution on Iraq did not constitute a declaration of war or equivalent action. The resolution stated: "The President is authorized to use the Armed Forces of the United States as he deems necessary and appropriate in order to 1) defend the national security of the United States against the continuing threat posed by Iraq; and 2) enforce all relevant United Nations Security Council resolutions regarding Iraq." The resolution unlawfully sought to delegate to the President the decision of whether or not to initiate a war against Iraq, based on whether he deemed it "necessary and appropriate." The Constitution does not allow Congress to delegate this exclusive power to the President, nor does it allow the President to seize this power.

In March 2003, the President launched a war against Iraq without any constitutional authority.

In all of these actions and decisions, President George W. Bush has acted in a manner contrary to his trust as President and Commander in Chief, and subversive of constitutional government, to the prejudice of the cause of law and justice and to the manifest injury of the people of the United

States. Wherefore, President George W. Bush, by such conduct, is guilty of an impeachable offense warranting removal from office.

Article VII notes

The United States Constitution, Article I, Section 8, Clause 11. http://www.house.gov/house/Constitution/Constitution.html

The Federalist No. 69, by Alexander Hamilton, 1788.

John Bonifaz, Warrior-King, *The Case for Impeaching George W. Bush*, with Foreword by Rep. John Conyers, Jr., Nation Books, New York, 2003.

Sen. Jacob K. Javits with Don Kellerman, *Who Makes War: The President versus Congress*, William Morrow & Company, Inc., New York, 1973.

John Hart Ely, *War and Responsibility: Constitutional Lessons of Vietnam and Its Aftermath*, Princeton University Press, Princeton, New Jersey, 1993.

Louis Fisher, *Presidential War Power*, University Press of Kansas, Lawrence, Kansas, 1995.

Article VIII

INVADING IRAQ, A SOVEREIGN NATION, IN VIOLATION OF THE UN CHARTER AND INTERNATIONAL CRIMINAL LAW

In his conduct while President of the United States, George W. Bush, in violation of his constitutional oath to faithfully execute the office of President of the United States and, to the best of his ability, preserve, protect, and defend the Constitution of the United States, and in violation of his constitutional duty under Article II, Section 3 of the Constitution "to take care that the laws be faithfully executed," violated United States law by invading the sovereign country of Iraq in violation of the United Nations Charter to wit:

(1) International Laws ratified by Congress are part of United States Law and must be followed as evidenced by the following:

(A) Article VI of the United States Constitution, which states "This Constitution, and the Laws of the United States which shall be made in Pursuance thereof; and all Treaties made, or which shall be made, under the Authority of the United States, shall be the supreme Law of the Land";

(2) The UN Charter, which entered into force following ratification by the United States in 1945, requires Security Council approval for the use of force except for self-defense against an armed attack as evidenced by the following:

A) Chapter 1, Article 2 of the United Nations Charter states:

"3. All Members shall settle their international disputes by peaceful means in such a manner that international peace and security, and justice, are not endangered.

"4. All Members shall refrain in their international relations from the threat or use of force against the territorial integrity or political independence of any state, or in any other manner inconsistent with the Purposes of the United Nations."

(B) Chapter 7, Article 51 of the United Nations Charter states:

"51. Nothing in the present Charter shall impair the inherent right of individual or collective self-defense if an armed attack occurs against a Member of the United Nations, until the Security Council has taken measures necessary to maintain international peace and security."

(3) There was no armed attack upon the United States by Iraq.

(4) The Security Council did not vote to approve the use of force against Iraq as evidenced by:

(A) A United Nation Press release which states that the United States had failed to convince the Security Council to approve the use of military force against Iraq. [UN]

(5) President Bush directed the United States military to invade Iraq on March 19th, 2003 in violation of the UN Charter and, therefore, in violation of United States Law as evidenced by the following:

(A) A letter from President Bush to Congress dated March 21st, 2003 stating "I directed US Armed Forces, operating with other coalition forces, to commence combat operations on March 19, 2003, against Iraq." [WH]

(B) On September 16, 2004 Kofi Annan, the Secretary General of the United Nations, speaking on the invasion, said, "I have indicated it was not in conformity with the UN charter. From our point of view, from the charter point of view, it was illegal." [BBC]

(C) The consequence of the instant and direction of President George W. Bush, in ordering an attack upon Iraq, a sovereign nation is in direct violation of United States Code, Title 18, Part 1, Chapter 118, Section 2441, governing the offense of war crimes.

(6). In the course of invading and occupying Iraq, the President, as Commander in Chief, has taken responsibility for the targeting of civilians, journalists, hospitals, and ambulances, use of antipersonnel weapons including cluster bombs in densely settled urban areas, the use of white phosphorous as a weapon, depleted uranium weapons, and the use of a new version of napalm found in Mark 77 firebombs. Under the direction of President George Bush the United States has engaged in collective punishment of Iraqi civilian populations, including but not limited to blocking roads, cutting electricity and water, destroying fuel stations, planting bombs in farm fields, demolishing houses, and plowing over orchards.

(A) Under the principle of "command responsibility," i.e., that a de jure command can be civilian as well as military, and can apply to the policy command of heads of state, said command brings President George Bush within the reach of international criminal law under the Additional Protocol I of June 8, 1977 to the Geneva Conventions of August 12, 1949, and Relating to the Protection of Victims of International Armed Conflicts, Article 86 (2). The United States is a state signatory to Additional Protocol I, on December 12, 1977.

(B) Furthermore, Article 85 (3) of said Protocol I defines as a grave breach making a civilian population or individual civilians the object of attacks. This offense, together with the principle of command responsibility, places President George Bush's conduct under the reach of the same law and principles described as the basis for war crimes prosecution at Nuremburg, under Article 6 of the Charter of the Nuremberg Tribunals: including crimes against peace, violations of the laws and customs of war and crimes against humanity, similarly codified in the Rome Statute of the International Criminal Court, Articles 5 through 8.

(C) The *Lancet* Report has established massive civilian casualties in Iraq as a result of the United States' invasion and occupation of that country.

(D) International laws governing wars of aggression are completely prohibited under the legal principle of jus cogens, whether or not a nation has signed or ratified a particular international agreement.

In all of these actions and decisions, President George W. Bush has acted in a manner contrary to his trust as President and Commander in Chief, and subversive of constitutional government, to the prejudice of the cause of law and justice and to the manifest injury of the people of the United States. Wherefore, President George W. Bush, by such conduct, is guilty of an impeachable offense warranting removal from office.

Article VIII notes

United States Constitution, Article VI. http://www.house.gov/house/Constitution/Constitution.html

All debts contracted and engagements entered into, before the adoption of this Constitution, shall be as valid against the United States under this Constitution, as under the Confederation.

This Constitution, and the laws of the United States which shall be made in pursuance thereof; and all treaties made, or which shall be made, under the authority of the United States, shall be the supreme law of the land; and the judges in every state shall be bound thereby, anything in the Constitution or laws of any State to the contrary notwithstanding.

The Senators and Representatives before mentioned, and the members of the several state legislatures, and all executive and judicial officers, both of the United States and of the several states, shall be bound by oath or affirmation, to support this Constitution; but no religious test shall ever be required as a qualification to any office or public trust under the United States.

The 35 Articles of Impeachment

United Nations Charter. http://www.un.org/aboutun/charter/index.html

Hans Blix statement, February 14, 2003. http://www.un.org/News/Press/docs/2003/sc7664.p2.doc.htm

El Baradei statement, March 7, 2003. http://www.un.org/News/Press/docs/2003/sc7682.doc.htm

United Nations Security Council statement, March 2003. http://www.un.org/News/Press/docs/2003/sc7696.doc.htm

White House statement, March 19, 2003. http://www.whitehouse.gov/news/releases/2003/03/20030321-5.html

Kofi Annan statement, September 16, 2004. http://news.bbc.co.uk/2/hi/middle_east/3661134.stm

Jackie Spinner, Karl Vick, and Omar Fekeiki, "US Forces Battle Into Heart of Fallujah," *The Washington Post*, November 10, 2004, page A01. http://www.washingtonpost.com/wp-dyn/articles/A35979-2004-Nov9_2.html

James W. Crawley, "Officials Confirm dropping Firebombs on Iraqi Troops, *San Diego Union-Tribune*, August 5, 2003. http://www.globalsecurity.org/org/news/2003/030805-firebombs01.htm

MK77 750lb Napalm, GlobalSecurity.org. http://www.globalsecurity.org/military/systems/munitions/mk77.htm

William M. Arkin, "America Cluster Bombs Iraq," *The Washington Post*, February 26, 2001. http://www.globalpolicy.org/security/issues/iraq/2001/0226cstr.htm .

UN Warns on Iraq Environment Fate, BBC, November 10, 2005. http://news.bbc.co.uk/1/hi/world/middle_east/4425562.stm

Larry Johnson, "Use of Depleted Uranium Weapons Lingers as Health Concern," *Seattle Post-Intelligencer*, August 4, 2003. http://seattlepi.nwsource.com/national/133581_du04.html

Convention Relative to the Protection of Civilian Persons in Time of War, August 12, 1949. http://www.yale.edu/lawweb/avalon/lawofwar/geneva07.htm

Article IX

FAILING TO PROVIDE TROOPS WITH BODY ARMOR
AND VEHICLE ARMOR

In his conduct while President of the United States, George W. Bush, in violation of his constitutional oath to faithfully execute the office of President of the United States and, to the best of his ability, preserve, protect, and defend the Constitution of the United States, and in violation of his constitutional duty under Article II, Section 3 of the Constitution "to take care that the laws be faithfully executed," has both personally and acting through his agents and subordinates, together with the Vice President, has been responsible for the deaths of members of the US military and serious injury and trauma to other soldiers, by failing to provide available body armor and vehicle armor.

While engaging in an invasion and occupation of choice, not fought in self-defense, and not launched in accordance with any timetable other than the President's choosing, President Bush sent US troops into danger without providing them with armor. This shortcoming has been known for years, during which time, the President has chosen to allow soldiers and Marines to continue to face unnecessary risk to life and limb rather then providing them with armor.

In all of these actions and decisions, President George W. Bush has acted in a manner contrary to his trust as President and Commander in Chief, and subversive of constitutional government, to the prejudice of the cause of law and justice and to the manifest injury of the people of the United States. Wherefore, President George W. Bush, by such conduct, is guilty of an impeachable offense warranting removal from office.

Article IX notes

Michael Moss, Extra Armor Could Have Saved Many Lives, *New York Times*, January 6, 2006. http://www.nytimes.com/2006/01/06/politics/06cnd-armor.html

John Diamond and Steven Komarow, "Humvee Vulnerabilities Raise Doubts on Future," USA Today, June 21, 2005. http://www.usatoday.com/news/washington/2005-06-21-iraq-armor_x.htm

Article X

FALSIFYING ACCOUNTS OF US TROOP DEATHS
AND INJURIES FOR POLITICAL PURPOSES

In his conduct while President of the United States, George W. Bush, in violation of his constitutional oath to faithfully execute the office of President of the United States and, to the best of his ability, preserve, protect, and defend the Constitution of the United States, and in violation of his constitutional duty under Article II, Section 3 of the Constitution "to take care that the laws be faithfully executed," has both personally and acting through his agents and subordinates, together with the Vice President, promoted false propaganda stories about members of the United States military, including individuals both dead and injured.

The White House and the Department of Defense (DOD) in 2004 promoted a false account of the death of Specialist Pat Tillman, reporting that he had died in a hostile exchange, delaying release of the information that he had died from friendly fire, shot in the forehead three times in a manner that led investigating doctors to believe he had been shot at close range.

A 2005 report by Brig. Gen. Gary M. Jones reported that in the days immediately following Specialist Tillman's death, US Army investigators were aware that Specialist Tillman was killed by friendly fire, shot three times to the head, and that senior Army commanders, including Gen. John Abizaid, knew of this fact within days of the shooting but nevertheless approved the awarding of the Silver Star, Purple Heart, and a posthumous promotion.

On April 24, 2007, Spc. Bryan O'Neal, the last soldier to see Specialist Pat Tillman alive, testified before the House Oversight and Government Reform Committee that he was warned by superiors not to divulge information that a fellow soldier killed Specialist Tillman, especially to the Tillman family. The White House refused to provide requested documents to the committee, citing "executive branch confidentiality interests."

The White House and DOD in 2003 promoted a false account of the injury of Jessica Dawn Lynch, reporting that she had been captured in a hostile exchange and had been dramatically rescued. On April 2, 2003, the DOD released a video of the rescue and claimed that Lynch had stab and bullet wounds, and that she had been slapped about on her hospital bed and interrogated. Iraqi doctors and nurses later interviewed, including Dr. Harith Al-Houssona, a doctor in the Nasirya hospital, described Lynch's injuries as "a broken arm, a broken thigh, and a dislocated ankle." According to Al-Houssona, there was no sign of gunshot or stab wounds, and Lynch's injuries were consistent with those that would be suffered in a car accident. Al-Houssona's claims were later confirmed in a US Army report leaked on July 10, 2003.

Lynch denied that she fought or was wounded fighting, telling Diane Sawyer that the Pentagon "used me to symbolize all this stuff. It's wrong. I don't know why they filmed [my rescue] or why they say these things.... I did not shoot, not a round, nothing. I went down praying to my knees. And that's the last I remember." She reported excellent treatment in Iraq, and that one person in the hospital even sang to her to help her feel at home.

On April 24, 2007 Lynch testified before the House Committee on Oversight and Government Reform:

"[Right after my capture], tales of great heroism were being told. My parent's home in Wirt County was under siege of the media all repeating the story of the little girl Rambo from the hills who went down fighting. It was not true.... I am still confused as to why they chose to lie."

The White House had heavily promoted the false story of Lynch's rescue, including in a speech by President Bush on April 28, 2003. After the fiction was exposed, the president awarded Lynch the Bronze Star.

In all of these actions and decisions, President George W. Bush has acted in a manner contrary to his trust as President and Commander in Chief, and subversive of constitutional government, to the prejudice of the cause of law and justice and to the manifest injury of the people of the United States. Wherefore, President George W. Bush, by such conduct, is guilty of an impeachable offense warranting removal from office.

Article X notes

Executive Summary, Attack on the 507th Maintenance Company, 23 March 2003, An Nasiriyah, Iraq. http://www.army.mil/features/507thMaintCmpy/AttackOnThe507MaintCmpy.pdf

Oversight Committee Holds Hearing on Tillman, Lynch Incidents. http://oversight.house.gov/story. asp?ID=1242

Kevin Tillman testimony, pp 15-25. http://oversight.house.gov/documents/20071114152054.pdf

The Tillman Fratricide: What the Leadership of the Defense Department Knew. http://oversight.house. gov/story.asp?ID=1415

Inspector General, "Review of Matters Related to the Death of Corporal Patrick Tillman, US Army." http:// www.defenselink.mil/home/pdf/Tillman_Redacted_Web_0307.pdf

http://abcnews.go.com/Primetime/Story?id=132433&page=1 Diane Sawyer interview with Jessica Lynch /a , ABC News, November 11, 2003.

Department of Defense, http://www.gwu.edu/~nsarchiv/NSAEBB/NSAEBB177/info_ops_roadmap.pdf" Information Operations Roadmap /a , October 30, 2003

Article XI

ESTABLISHMENT OF PERMANENT
US MILITARY BASES IN IRAQ

In his conduct while President of the United States, George W. Bush, in violation of his constitutional oath to faithfully execute the office of President of the United States and, to the best of his ability, preserve, protect, and defend the Constitution of the United States, and in violation of his constitutional duty under Article II, Section 3 of the Constitution "to take care that the laws be faithfully executed," has violated an act of Congress that he himself signed into law by using public funds to construct permanent US military bases in Iraq.

On January 28, 2008, President George W. Bush signed into law the National Defense Authorization Act for Fiscal Year 2008 (H.R. 4986). Noting that the Act "authorizes funding for the defense of the United States and its interests abroad, for military construction, and for national security-related energy programs," the president added the following "signing statement":

"Provisions of the Act, including sections 841, 846, 1079, and 1222, purport to impose requirements that could inhibit the President's ability to carry out his constitutional obligations to take care that the laws be faithfully executed, to protect national security, to supervise the executive branch, and to execute his authority as Commander in Chief. The executive branch shall construe such provisions in a manner consistent with the constitutional authority of the President."

Section 1222 clearly prohibits the expenditure of money for the purpose of establishing permanent US military bases in Iraq. The construction of over $1 billion in US military bases in Iraq, including runways for aircraft, continues despite Congressional intent, as the Administration intends to force upon the Iraqi government such terms which will assure the bases remain in Iraq.

Iraqi officials have informed members of Congress in May 2008 of the strong opposition within the Iraqi parliament and throughout Iraq to the agreement that the administration is trying to negotiate with Iraqi Prime Minister Nouri al-Maliki. The agreement seeks to assure a long-term US presence in Iraq of which military bases are the most obvious, sufficient and necessary construct, thus clearly defying Congressional intent as to the matter and meaning of "permanency."

In all of these actions and decisions, President George W. Bush has acted in a manner contrary to his trust as President and Commander in Chief, and subversive of constitutional government, to the prejudice of the cause of law and justice and to the manifest injury of the people of the United States. Wherefore, President George W. Bush, by such conduct, is guilty of an impeachable offense warranting removal from office.

Article XI notes

Tom Engelhardt, "Iraq as a Pentagon Construction Site," December 2, 2007. http://tomdispatch.com/post/174869/a_basis_for_enduring_relationships_in_iraq

"House Votes to Ban Permanent Bases in Iraq," *The Gavel*, July 25, 2007. http://www.speaker.gov/blog/?p=621

Spencer Ackerman, "War Czar: Permanent Iraq Bases Won't Require Senate Ratification," *TPM Muckraker*, November 26, 2007. http://www.tpmmuckraker.com/archives/004776.php

"Extended Presence of US in Iraq Looms Large," Associated Press, March 21, 2006. http://www.msnbc.msn.com/id/11072377

Tom Engelhardt, "Can You Say "Permanent Bases?," February 14, 2006. http://www.tomdispatch.com/post/59774/a_permanent_basis_for_withdrawal

Iraq Facilities, Global Security. http://www.globalsecurity.org/military/facility/iraq-intro.htm

"If the US is Ultimately Leaving Iraq, Why is the Military Building 'Permanent' Bases?," Friends Committee on National Legislation, February 20, 2008. http://www.fcnl.org/iraq/bases.htm

Gareth Porter, Inter Press Service, Bush Pledges on Iraq Bases Pact Were a Ruse, June 13, 2008. http://www.afterdowningstreet.org/node/34098

Article XII

INITIATING A WAR AGAINST IRAQ FOR CONTROL
OF THAT NATION'S NATURAL RESOURCES

In his conduct while President of the United States, George W. Bush, in violation of his constitutional oath to faithfully execute the office of President of the United States and, to the best of his ability, preserve, protect, and defend the Constitution of the United States, and in violation of his constitutional duty under Article II, Section 3 of the Constitution "to take care that the laws be faithfully executed," has both personally and acting through his agents and subordinates, together with the Vice President, invaded and occupied a foreign nation for the purpose, among other purposes, of seizing control of that nation's oil.

The White House and its representatives in Iraq have, since the occupation of Baghdad began, attempted to gain control of Iraqi oil. This effort has included pressuring the new Iraqi government to pass a hydrocarbon law. Within weeks of the fall of Saddam Hussein in 2003, the US Agency for International Development (USAid) awarded a $240 million contract to Bearing Point, a private US company. A Bearing Point employee, based in the US embassy in Baghdad, was hired to advise the Iraqi Ministry of Oil on drawing up the new hydrocarbon law. The draft law places executives of foreign oil companies on a council with the task of approving their own contracts with Iraq; it denies the Iraqi National Oil Company exclusive rights for the exploration, development, production, transportation, and marketing of Iraqi oil, and allows foreign companies to control Iraqi oil fields containing 80 percent of Iraqi oil for up to 35 years through contracts that can remain secret for up to two months. The draft law itself contains secret appendices.

President Bush provided unrelated reasons for the invasion of Iraq to the public and Congress, but those reasons have been established to have been categorically fraudulent, as evidenced by the herein mentioned Articles of Impeachment I, II, III, IV, VI, and VII.

Parallel to the development of plans for war against Iraq, the US State Department's Future of Iraq project, begun as early as April 2002, involved meetings in Washington and London of 17 working groups, each composed of 10 to 20 Iraqi exiles and international experts selected by the State Department. The Oil and Energy working group met four times between December 2002 and April 2003. Ibrahim Bahr al-Uloum, later the Iraqi Oil Minister, was a member of the group, which concluded that Iraq "should be opened to international oil companies as quickly as possible after the war," and that, "the country should establish a conducive business environment to attract investment of oil and gas resources." The same group recommended production-sharing agreements with foreign oil companies, the same approach found in the draft hydrocarbon law, and control over Iraq's oil resources remains a prime objective of the Bush Administration.

Prior to his election as Vice President, Dick Cheney, then-CEO of Halliburton, in a speech at the Institute of Petroleum in 1999 demonstrated a keen awareness of the sensitive economic and geopolitical role of Midde East oil resources saying: "By 2010, we will need on the order of an additional 50 million barrels a day. So where is the oil going to come from? Governments and national oil companies are obviously controlling about 90 percent of the assets. Oil remains fundamentally a government business. While many regions of the world offer great oil opportunities, the Middle East, with two-thirds of the world's oil and lowest cost, is still where the prize ultimately lies. Even though companies are anxious for greater access there, progress continues to be slow."

The Vice President led the work of a secret energy task force, as described in Article XXXII below, a task force that focused on, among other things, the acquisition of Iraqi oil through developing a controlling private corporate interest in said oil.

In all of these actions and decisions, President George W. Bush has acted in a manner contrary to his trust as President and Commander in Chief, and subversive of constitutional government, to the prejudice of the cause of law and justice and to the manifest injury of the people of the United States. Wherefore, President George W. Bush, by such conduct, is guilty of an impeachable offense warranting removal from office.

Article XII notes

Congressman Dennis Kucinich Floor Speech, May 2007. http://afterdowningstreet.org/node/33220

Energy Task Force Map of Iraq. http://www.judicialwatch.org/IraqOilMap.pdf

US Senate, Democratic Policy Committee, "Two US Government Inspectors General Conclude: Bush Administration's Contracting Process in Iraq Still Plagued by Overruns, May 24, 2004. http://democrats. senate.gov/dpc/dpc-new.cfm?doc_name=op-108-2-88

Stephen Foley, "Shock and Oil: Iraq's Billions & the White House Connection," The Independent, January 14, 2007. http://www.independent.co.uk/news/world/americas/shock-and-oil-iraqs-billions-amp-the-white-house-connection-431977.html

Antonia Juhasz, "Whose Oil is it Anyway?," New York Times, March 13, 2007. http://www.nytimes. com/2007/03/13/opinion/13juhasz.html

Munir Chalabi, Political Comments on the Draft of the Iraqi Oil Law, March 15, 2007. http://www.zmag. org/znet/viewArticle/1833

Dick Cheney, a href="http://www.energybulletin.net/559.html" Full Text of Dick Cheney's Speech /a at the Institute of Petroleum Autumn Lunch, 1999, Published on June 8, 2004 by the London Institute of Petroleum (last visited May 16, 2008).

National Security Archive, "New State Department Releases on the 'Future of Iraq' Project," September 1, 2006 http://www.gwu.edu/~nsarchiv/NSAEBB/NSAEBB198/index.htm

Greg Muttitt, "Crude Designs: The Rip-Off of Iraq's Oil Wealth," Platform, November 2005. http://www. crudedesigns.org

Hassan Hafidh, A href="http://www.rigzone.com/news/article.asp?a_id=38840" Iraq's Draft Hydrocarbon Law Recommends PSA's /a , Dow Jones Newswires, December 6, 2006 (last visited May 16, 2008).

ARTICLE XIII

CREATING A SECRET TASK FORCE TO DEVELOP ENERGY
AND MILITARY POLICIES WITH RESPECT TO IRAQ
AND OTHER COUNTRIES

In his conduct while President of the United States, George W. Bush, in violation of his constitutional oath to faithfully execute the office of President of the United States and, to the best of his ability, preserve, protect, and defend the Constitution of the United States, and in violation of his constitutional duty to take care that the laws be faithfully executed, has both personally and acting through his agents and subordinates, together with the Vice President, created a secret task force to guide our nation's energy policy and military policy, and undermined Congress' ability to legislate by thwarting attempts to investigate the nature of that policy.

A Government Accountability Office (GAO) Report on the Cheney Energy Task Force, in August 2003, described the creation of this task force as follows:

"In a January 29, 2001, memorandum, the President established NEPDG [the National Energy Policy Development Group] — comprised of the Vice President, nine cabinet-level officials, and four other senior administration officials — to gather information, deliberate, and make recommendations to the President by the end of fiscal year 2001. The President called on the Vice President to chair the group, direct its work and, as necessary, establish subordinate working groups to assist NEPDG."

The four "other senior administration officials were the Director of the Office of Management and Budget, the Assistant to the President and Deputy Chief of Staff for Policy, the Assistant to the President for Economic Policy, and the Deputy Assistant to the President for Intergovernmental Affairs."

The GAO report found that:

"In developing the National Energy Policy report, the NEPDG Principals, Support Group, and participating agency officials and staff met with,

47

solicited input from, or received information and advice from nonfederal energy stakeholders, principally petroleum, coal, nuclear, natural gas, and electricity industry representatives and lobbyists. The extent to which submissions from any of these stakeholders were solicited, influenced policy deliberations, or were incorporated into the final report cannot be determined based on the limited information made available to GAO. NEPDG met and conducted its work in two distinct phases: the first phase culminated in a March 19, 2001, briefing to the President on challenges relating to energy supply and the resulting economic impact; the second phase ended with the May 16, 2001, presentation of the final report to the President. The Office of the Vice President's (OVP) unwillingness to provide the NEPDG records or other related information precluded GAO from fully achieving its objectives and substantially limited GAO's ability to comprehensively analyze the NEPDG records associated with that process.

"None of the key federal entities involved in the NEPDG effort provided GAO with a complete accounting of the costs that they incurred during the development of the National Energy Policy report. The two federal entities responsible for funding the NEPDG effort—OVP and the Department of Energy (DOE)—did not provide the comprehensive cost information that GAO requested. OVP provided GAO with 77 pages of information, two-thirds of which contained no cost information while the remaining one-third contained some miscellaneous information of little to no usefulness. OVP stated that it would not provide any additional information. DOE, the Department of the Interior, and the Environmental Protection Agency (EPA) provided GAO with estimates of certain costs and salaries associated with the NEPDG effort, but these estimates, all calculated in different ways, were not comprehensive."

In 2003, the Commerce Department disclosed a partial collection of materials from the NEPDG, including documents, maps, and charts, dated March 2001, of Iraq's, Saudi Arabia's and the United Arab Emirates' oil fields, pipelines, refineries, tanker terminals, and development projects.

On November 16, 2005, the *Washington Post* reported on a White House document showing that oil company executives had met with the NEPDG, something that some of those same executives had just that week denied in Congressional testimony. The Bush Administration had not corrected the inaccurate testimony.

On July 18, 2007, the *Washington Post* reported the full list of names of those who had met with the NEPDG.

In 1998 Kenneth Derr, then chief executive of Chevron, told a San Francisco audience, "Iraq possesses huge reserves of oil and gas, reserves I'd love Chevron to have access to." According to the GAO report, Chevron provided detailed advice to the NEPDG.

In March, 2001, the NEPDG recommended that the United States Government support initiatives by Middle Eastern countries "to open up areas of their energy sectors to foreign investment." Following the invasion of Iraq, the United States has pressured the new Iraqi parliament to pass a hydrocarbon law that would do exactly that. The draft law, if passed, would take the majority of Iraq's oil out of the exclusive hands of the Iraqi Government and open it to international oil companies for a generation or more. The Bush administration hired Bearing Point, a US company, to help write the law in 2004. It was submitted to the Iraqi Council of Representatives in May 2007.

In all of these actions and decisions, President George W. Bush has acted in a manner contrary to his trust as President and Commander in Chief, and subversive of constitutional government, to the prejudice of the cause of law and justice and to the manifest injury of the people of the United States. Wherefore, President George W. Bush, by such conduct, is guilty of an impeachable offense warranting removal from office.

Article XIII notes

National Energy Policy, 2001. http://www.whitehouse.gov/energy/2001/index.html

Government Accountability Office, Report on Cheney Energy Task Force, August 2003. http://oversight. house.gov/documents/20040625102432-06243.pdf

Congressman Dennis Kucinich floor speech, May 2007. http://afterdowningstreet.org/node/33220

Dana Milbank and Justin Blum, "Document Says Oil Chiefs Met With Cheney Task Force, *Washington Post*, November 16, 2005. http://www.washingtonpost.com/wp-dyn/content/article/2005/11/15/AR2005111501842.html

Energy Task Force Map of Iraq. http://www.judicialwatch.org/IraqOilMap.pdf

Energy Task Force Meeting Participants. http://www.washingtonpost.com/wp-srv/politics/documents/cheney_energy_task_force.html

Article XIV

MISPRISION OF A FELONY, MISUSE AND EXPOSURE OF CLASSIFIED INFORMATION AND OBSTRUCTION OF JUSTICE IN THE MATTER OF VALERIE PLAME WILSON, CLANDESTINE AGENT OF THE CENTRAL INTELLIGENCE AGENCY

In his conduct while President of the United States, George W. Bush, in violation of his constitutional oath to faithfully execute the office of President of the United States and, to the best of his ability, preserve, protect, and defend the Constitution of the United States, and in violation of his constitutional duty under Article II, Section 3 of the Constitution "to take care that the laws be faithfully executed," has both personally and acting through his agents and subordinates, together with the Vice President,

(1) suppressed material information;

(2) selectively declassified information for the improper purposes of retaliating against a whistleblower and presenting a misleading picture of the alleged threat from Iraq;

(3) facilitated the exposure of the identity of Valerie Plame Wilson who had theretofore been employed as a covert CIA operative;

(4) failed to investigate the improper leaks of classified information from within his administration;

(5) failed to cooperate with an investigation into possible federal violations resulting from this activity; and

(6) finally, entirely undermined the prosecution by commuting the sentence of Lewis Libby citing false and insubstantial grounds, all in an effort to prevent Congress and the citizens of the United States from discovering the deceitful nature of the President's claimed justifications for the invasion of Iraq.

In facilitating this exposure of classified information and the subsequent cover-up, in all of these actions and decisions, President George W. Bush has acted in a manner contrary to his trust as President, and subversive of constitutional government, to the prejudice of the cause of law and justice and to the manifest injury of the people of the United States. Wherefore, President George W. Bush, by such conduct, is guilty of an impeachable offense warranting removal from office.

Article XIV notes

Murray Waas, "Bush Directed Cheney To Counter War Critic," *National Journal*, July 3, 2006. http://news.nationaljournal.com/articles/0703nj1.htm

Elizabeth de la Vega, "Final Jeopardy," TomDispatch.com, April 9, 2006. http://www.tomdispatch.com/post/76008/de_la_vega_on_the_president_s_final_jeopardy_question

Letter from Representative Henry Waxman to then White House Chief of Staff Andrew Card, July 14, 2005. http://oversight.house.gov/documents/20050714122956-30175.pdf

Letter from Representative Henry Waxman to White House Chief of Staff Joshua Bolten, March 16, 2007. http://oversight.house.gov/documents/20070316154127-11403.pdf

Letter from Representative Henry Waxman to Attorney General Michael Mukasey, December 3, 2007. http://oversight.house.gov/documents/20071203103022.pdf

Jon Ponder, "Did Bush Lie to Federal Investigators in the CIA Leak Case?," *Pensito Review*, November 21, 2007. http://www.pensitoreview.com/2007/11/21/did-bush-lie-to-fitzgerald-too1

Scott McClellan, *What Happened: Inside the Bush White House and Washington's Culture of Deception*, 2008.

Article XV

PROVIDING IMMUNITY FROM PROSECUTION
FOR CRIMINAL CONTRACTORS IN IRAQ

In his conduct while President of the United States, George W. Bush, in violation of his constitutional oath to faithfully execute the office of President of the United States and, to the best of his ability, preserve, protect, and defend the Constitution of the United States, and in violation of his constitutional duty under Article II, Section 3 of the Constitution "to take care that the laws be faithfully executed," has both personally and acting through his agents and subordinates, together with the Vice President, established policies granting United States government contractors and their employees in Iraq immunity from Iraqi law, US law, and international law.

Lewis Paul Bremer III, then-Director of Reconstruction and Humanitarian Assistance for post-war Iraq, on June 27, 2004, issued Coalition Provisional Authority Order Number 17, which granted members of the US military, US mercenaries, and other US contractor employees immunity from Iraqi law.

The Bush Administration has chosen not to apply the Uniform Code of Military Justice or United States law to mercenaries and other contractors employed by the United States government in Iraq.

Operating free of Iraqi or US law, mercenaries have killed many Iraqi civilians in a manner that observers have described as aggression and not as self-defense. Many US contractors have also alleged that they have been the victims of aggression (in several cases of rape) by their fellow contract employees in Iraq. These charges have not been brought to trial, and in several cases the contracting companies and the US State Department have worked together in attempting to cover them up.

Under the Fourth Geneva Convention, to which the United States is party, and which under Article VI of the US Constitution is therefore the supreme law of the United States, it is the responsibility of an occupying force to ensure the protection and human rights of the civilian population.

The efforts of President Bush and his subordinates to attempt to establish a lawless zone in Iraq are in violation of the law.

In all of these actions and decisions, President George W. Bush has acted in a manner contrary to his trust as President and subversive of constitutional government, to the prejudice of the cause of law and justice and to the manifest injury of the people of the United States. Wherefore, President George W. Bush, by such conduct, is guilty of an impeachable offense warranting removal from office.

Article XV notes

Coalition Provisional Authority, Order Number 17. http://www.cpairaq.org/regulations/20040627_
CPAORD_17_Status_of_Coalition__Rev__with_Annex_A.pdf

The Fourth Geneva Convention. http://www.icrc.org/ihl.nsf/CONVPRES?OpenView

April 2006 Video of President Bush. http://www.youtube.com/watch?v=kO3Wob0WoIM

Joanne Mariner, "Private Contractors Who Torture," FindLaw, May 10, 2004. http://writ.news.findlaw.com/
mariner/20040510.html

Ammar Karim, Middle East Online, October 24, 2007. http://www.middle-east-online.com/
english/?id=22791

Massimo Calabresi, "Will Contractors Lose Iraq Immunity?," *Time* magazine, February 13, 2008. http://
www.time.com/time/nation/article/0,8599,1712938,00.html

Ellen McCarthy, "Immunity Provision Extended for US Firms With Reconstruction Contracts," *Washington
Post*, page A18, June 29, 2004. http://www.washingtonpost.com/wp-dyn/articles/A13297-2004-
Jun28.html?referrer=emailarticle

Iraq to End Contractor Immunity, BBC, October 30, 2007. http://news.bbc.co.uk/1/hi/world/middle_
east/7069173.stm

Alex Koppelman and Mark Benjamin, "What happens to private contractors who kill Iraqis? Maybe Nothing," *Salon*, September 18, 2007. http://www.salon.com/news/feature/2007/09/18/blackwater

John Byrne and Gavin McNett, "US Quietly Demands Iraq Give Defense Contractors US Military Immunity
from Prosecution," RawStory, January 25, 2008. http://rawstory.com/news/2007/US_quietly_de-
mands_Iraq_give_defense_0125.html

Article XVI

RECKLESS MISSPENDING AND WASTE OF US TAX DOLLARS IN CONNECTION WITH IRAQ CONTRACTORS

In his conduct while President of the United States, George W. Bush, in violation of his constitutional oath to faithfully execute the office of President of the United States and, to the best of his ability, preserve, protect, and defend the Constitution of the United States, and in violation of his constitutional duty under Article II, Section 3 of the Constitution "to take care that the laws be faithfully executed," has both personally and acting through his agents and subordinates, together with the Vice President, recklessly wasted public funds on contracts awarded to close associates, including companies guilty of defrauding the government in the past, contracts awarded without competitive bidding, "cost-plus" contracts designed to encourage cost overruns, and contracts not requiring satisfactory completion of the work. These failures have been the rule, not the exception, in the awarding of contracts for work in the United States and abroad over the past seven years. Repeated exposure of fraud and waste has not been met by the president with correction of systemic problems, but rather with retribution against whistleblowers.

The House Committee on Oversight and Government Reform reported on Iraq reconstruction contracting:

"From the beginning, the Administration adopted a flawed contracting approach in Iraq. Instead of maximizing competition, the Administration opted to award no-bid, cost-plus contracts to politically connected contractors. Halliburton's secret $7 billion contract to restore Iraq's oil infrastructure is the prime example. Under this no-bid, cost-plus contract, Halliburton was reimbursed for its costs and then received an additional fee, which was a percentage of its costs. This created an incentive for Halliburton to run up its costs in order to increase its potential profit.

"Even after the Administration claimed it was awarding Iraq contracts competitively in early 2004, real price competition was missing. Iraq was divided geographically and by economic sector into a handful of fiefdoms. Individual contractors were then awarded monopoly contracts for all of the work within given fiefdoms. Because these monopoly contracts were awarded before specific projects were identified, there was no actual price competition for more than 2,000 projects.

"In the absence of price competition, rigorous government oversight becomes essential for accountability. Yet the Administration turned much of the contract oversight work over to private companies with blatant conflicts of interest. Oversight contractors oversaw their business partners and, in some cases, were placed in a position to assist their own construction work under separate monopoly construction contracts....

"Under Halliburton's two largest Iraq contracts, Pentagon auditors found $1 billion in 'questioned' costs and over $400 million in 'unsupported' costs. Former Halliburton employees testified that the company charged $45 for cases of soda, billed $100 to clean 15- pound bags of laundry, and insisted on housing its staff as the five-star Kempinski hotel in Kuwait. Halliburton truck drivers testified that the company 'torched' brand new $85,000 trucks rather than perform relatively minor repairs and regular maintenance. Halliburton procurement officials described the company's informal motto in Iraq as 'Don't worry about price. It's cost-plus.' A Halliburton manager was indicted for 'major fraud against the United States' for allegedly billing more than $5.5 billion for work that should have cost only $685,000 in exchange for a $1 million kickback from a Kuwaiti subcontractor....

"The Air Force found that another US government contractor, Custer Battles, set up shell subcontractors to inflate prices. Those overcharges were passed along to the U.S government under the company's cost-plus contract to provide security for Baghdad International Airport. In one case, the company allegedly took Iraqi-owned forklifts, re-painted them, and leased them to the US government.

"Despite the spending of billions of taxpayer dollars, US reconstruction efforts in keys sectors of the Iraqi economy are failing. Over two years after the US-led invasion of Iraq, oil and electricity production has fallen below pre-war levels. The Administration has failed to even measure how many Iraqis lack access to drinkable water."

Constitution in Crisis, a book by Congressman John Conyers, details the Bush Administration's response when contract abuse is made public:

"Bunnatine Greenhouse was the chief contracting officer at the Army Corps of Engineers, the agency that has managed much of the reconstruction work in Iraq. In October 2004, Ms. Greenhouse came forward and revealed that top Pentagon officials showed improper favoritism to Halliburton when awarding military contracts to Halliburton subsidiary Kellogg Brown & Root (KBR). Greenhouse stated that when the Pentagon awarded Halliburton a five-year $7 billion contract, it pressured her to withdraw her objections, actions which she claimed were unprecedented in her experience.

"On June 27, 2005, Ms. Greenhouse testified before Congress, detailing that the contract award process was compromised by improper influence by political appointees, participation by Halliburton officials in meetings where bidding requirements were discussed, and a lack of competition. She stated that the Halliburton contracts represented "the most blatant and improper contract abuse I have witnessed during the course of my professional career." Days before the hearing, the acting general counsel of the Army Corps of Engineers paid Ms. Greenhouse a visit and reportedly let it be known that it would not be in her best interest to appear voluntarily.

"On August 27, 2005, the Army demoted Ms. Greenhouse, removing her from the elite Senior Executive Service and transferring her to a lesser job in the corps' civil works division . As Frank Rich of The *New York Times* described the situation, '[H]er crime was not obstructing justice but pursuing it by vehemently questioning irregularities in the awarding of some $7 billion worth of no-bid contracts in Iraq to the Halliburton subsidiary Kellogg Brown Root.' The demotion was in apparent retaliation for her speaking out against the abuses, even though she previously had stellar reviews and over 20 years of experience in military procurement."

The House Committee on Oversight and Government Reform reports on domestic contracting:

"The Administration's domestic contracting record is no better than its record on Iraq. Waste, fraud, and abuse appear to be the rule rather than the exception....

"A Transportation Security Administration (TSA) cost-plus contract with NCS Pearson, Inc., to hire federal airport screeners was plagued by poor management and egregious waste. Pentagon auditors challenged $303 million (over 40%) of the $741 million spent by Pearson under the contract. The auditors detailed numerous concerns with the charges of Pearson and its subcontractors, such as '$20-an-hour temporary workers billed to the government at $48 per hour, subcontractors who signed out $5,000 in cash at a time with no supporting documents, $377,273.75 in unsubstantiated long distance phone calls, $514,201 to rent tents that flooded in a rainstorm, [and] $4.4 million in "no show" fees for job candidates who did not appear for tests." A Pearson employee who supervised Pearson's hiring efforts at 43 sites in the US described the contract as 'a waste a taxpayer's money.' The CEO of one Pearson subcontractor paid herself $5.4 million for nine months work and provided herself with a $270,000 pension....

"The Administration is spending $239 million on the Integrated Surveillance and Intelligence System, a no-bid contract to provide thousands of cameras and sensors to monitor activity on the Mexican and Canadian borders. Auditors found that the contractor, International Microwave Corp., billed for work it never did and charged for equipment it never provided, 'creat[ing] a potential for overpayments of almost $13 million.' Moreover, the border monitoring system reportedly does not work....

"After spending more than $4.5 billion on screening equipment for the nation's entry points, the Department of Homeland Security is now 'moving to replace or alter much of' it because 'it is ineffective, unreliable or too expensive to operate.' For example, radiation monitors at ports and borders reportedly could not 'differentiate between radiation emitted by a nuclear bomb and naturally occurring radiation from everyday material like cat litter or ceramic tile.'...

"The TSA awarded Boeing a cost-plus contract to install over 1,000 explosive detection systems for airline passenger luggage. After installation, the machines 'began to register false alarms' and '[s]creeners were forced to open and hand-check bags.' To reduce the number of false alarms, the sensitivity of the machines was lowered, which reduced the effectiveness of the detectors. Despite these serious problems, Boeing received an $82 million profit that the Inspector General determined to be 'excessive.'...

"The FBI spent $170 million on a 'Virtual Case File' system that does not operate as required. After three years of work under a cost-plus contract failed to produce a functional system, the FBI scrapped the program and began work on the new 'Sentinel' Case File System....

"The Department of Homeland Security Inspector General found that taxpayer dollars were being lavished on perks for agency officials. One IG report found that TSA spent over $400,000 on its first leader's executive office suite. Another found that TSA spent $350,000 on a gold-plated gym....

"According to news reports, Pentagon auditors ... examined a contract between the Transportation Security Administration (TSA) and Unisys, a technology and consulting company, for the upgrade of airport computer networks. Among other irregularities, government auditors found that Unisys may have overbilled for as much as 171,000 hours of labor and overtime by charging for employees at up to twice their actual rate of compensation. While the cost ceiling for the contract was set at $1 billion, Unisys has reportedly billed the government $940 million with more than half of the seven-year contract remaining and more than half of the TSA-monitored airports still lacking upgraded networks."

In all of these actions and decisions, President George W. Bush has acted in a manner contrary to his trust as President, and subversive of constitutional government, to the prejudice of the cause of law and justice and to the manifest injury of the people of the United States. Wherefore, President George W. Bush, by such conduct, is guilty of an impeachable offense warranting removal from office.

Article XVI notes

The House Committee on Oversight and Government Reform on Iraq Reconstruction Contracting. http://oversight.house.gov/itsyourmoney/iraq.html

Congressman John Conyers, *The Constitution in Crisis*. http://afterdowningstreet.org/constitutionincrisis

The House Committee on Oversight and Government Reform on Domestic Contracting. http://oversight.house.gov/itsyourmoney/homeland_security.html

Senator Barack Obama, "Statement of Senator Barack Obama on his Amendment to Stop No-bid Contracts for Gulf Coast Recovery & Reconstruction, May 2, 2006." http://obama.senate.gov/speech/060502-statement_of_se_5

Oliver Morgan, Congress Probes Hurricane Clean Up Contracts, *The Observer*, September 11, 2005. http://www.guardian.co.uk/business/2005/sep/11/hurricanekatrina.usnews

Farah Stockman, "US firms Suspected of Bilking Iraq Funds: Millions Missing from Program for Rebuilding, Boston.com World News, April 16, 2006. http://www.boston.com/news/world/articles/2006/04/16/us_firms_suspected_of_bilking_iraq_funds

Adam Zagorin & Timothy J. Burger, "Beyond the Call of Duty," Time.com, May 18, 2008. http://www.time.com/time/magazine/article/0,9171,733760,00.html

Article XVII

ILLEGAL DETENTION: DETAINING INDEFINITELY AND WITHOUT CHARGE PERSONS BOTH US CITIZENS AND FOREIGN CAPTIVES

In his conduct while President of the United States, George W. Bush, in violation of his constitutional oath to faithfully execute the office of President of the United States and, to the best of his ability, preserve, protect, and defend the Constitution of the United States, and in violation of his constitutional duty under Article II, Section 3 of the Constitution "to take care that the laws be faithfully executed," has both personally and acting through his agents and subordinates, together with the Vice President, violated United States and International Law and the US Constitution by illegally detaining indefinitely and without charge persons both US citizens and foreign captives.

In a statement on Feb. 7, 2002, President Bush declared that in the US fight against Al Qaeda, "none of the provisions of Geneva apply," thus rejecting the Geneva Conventions that protect captives in wars and other conflicts. By that time, the administration was already transporting captives from the war in Afghanistan, both alleged Al Qaeda members and supporters, and also Afghans accused of being fighters in the army of the Taliban government, to US-run prisons in Afghanistan and to the detention facility at Guantanamo Bay, Cuba. The round-up and detention without charge of Muslim non-citizens inside the US began almost immediately after the September 11, 2001 attacks on the World Trade Center and the Pentagon, with some being held as long as nine months. The US, on orders of the president, began capturing and detaining without charge alleged terror suspects in other countries and detaining them abroad and at the US Naval base in Guantanamo.

Many of these detainees have been subjected to systematic abuse, including beatings, which have been subsequently documented by news reports, photographic evidence, testimony in Congress, lawsuits, and in the case of detainees in the US, by an investigation conducted by the Justice Department's Office of the Inspector General.

In violation of US law and the Geneva Conventions, the Bush Administration instructed the Department of Justice and the US Department of Defense to refuse to provide the identities or locations of these detainees, despite requests from Congress and from attorneys for the detainees. The president even declared the right to detain US citizens indefinitely, without charge and without providing them access to counsel or the courts, thus depriving them of their constitutional and basic human rights. Several of those US citizens were held in military brigs in solitary confinement for as long as three years before being either released or transferred to civilian detention.

Detainees in US custody in Iraq and Guantanamo have, in violation of the Geneva Conventions, been hidden from and denied visits by the International Red Cross organization, while thousands of others in Iraq, Guantanamo, Afghanistan, ships in foreign off-shore sites, and an unknown number of so-called "black sites" around the world have been denied any opportunity to challenge their detentions. The president, acting on his own claimed authority, has declared the hundreds of detainees at Guantanamo Bay to be "enemy combatants" not subject to US law and not even subject to military law, but nonetheless potentially liable to the death penalty.

The detention of individuals without due process violates the 5th Amendment. While the Bush administration has been rebuked in several court cases, most recently that of Ali al-Marri, it continues to attempt to exceed constitutional limits.

In all of these actions violating US and International law, President George W. Bush has acted in a manner contrary to his trust as President and Commander in Chief, and subversive of constitutional government, to the prejudice of the cause of law and justice and to the manifest injury of the people of the United States. Wherefore, President George W. Bush, by such conduct, is guilty of an impeachable offense warranting removal from office.

Article XVII

Gonzales Memo. http://www.humanrightsfirst.org/us_law/etn/gonzales/memos_dir/memo_20020801_JD_%20Gonz_.pdf

Stephen Grey, "America's Gulag," *The New Statesman*, May 17, 2004. http://www.newstatesman.com/200405170016

Article XVII

Steven R. Weisman, "US Rebuffs Red Cross Request for Access to Detainees Held in Secret," *New York Times*, December 10, 2005. http://www.nytimes.com/2005/12/10/politics/10detain.html

US Constitution. Amendment V.

"No person shall be held to answer for a capital, or otherwise infamous crime, unless on a presentment or indictment of a Grand Jury, except in cases arising in the land or naval forces, or in the Militia, when in actual service in time of War or public danger; nor shall any person be subject for the same offense to be twice put in jeopardy of life or limb; nor shall be compelled in any criminal case to be a witness against himself, nor be deprived of life, liberty, or property, without due process of law; nor shall private property be taken for public use, without just compensation."

Oscar Uhler et al., Geneva Convention IV: ICRC Commentary 51 (1958); Geneva Convention IV, art. 4(1) & 4(3); Protocol Additional to the Geneva Conventions of 12 August 1949, and Relating to the Protection of Victims of International Armed Conflicts (Protocol I), art. 50, 1125 U.N.T.S. 3 (1977); FM 27-10 ¶ 73.

Article 118 of Third Geneva Convention states that "prisoners of war shall be released and repatriated without delay after the cessation of active hostilities." Third Geneva Convention, supra note 15, Art. 118. Article 134 of the Fourth Geneva Convention requires parties to "endeavour, upon the close of hostilities or occupation, to ensure the return of all internees to their last place of residence, or to facilitate their repatriation." Fourth Geneva Convention, supra note 15, Art. 134. Thus, repatriation of detainees upon cessation of hostilities is mandated by the Geneva Conventions.

Jean S. Pictet (ed.), Geneva Convention Relative to the Treatment of Prisoners of War: Commentary, ICRC, Geneva, 1960, 543.

Article XVIII

TORTURE: SECRETLY AUTHORIZING, AND ENCOURAGING THE USE OF TORTURE AGAINST CAPTIVES IN AFGHANISTAN, IRAQ, AND OTHER PLACES, AS A MATTER OF OFFICIAL POLICY

In his conduct while President of the United States, George W. Bush, in violation of his constitutional oath to faithfully execute the office of President of the United States and, to the best of his ability, preserve, protect, and defend the Constitution of the United States, and in violation of his constitutional duty under Article II, Section 3 of the Constitution "to take care that the laws be faithfully executed," has both personally and acting through his agents and subordinates, together with the Vice President, violated United States and International Law and the US Constitution by secretly authorizing and encouraging the use of torture against captives in Afghanistan, Iraq in connection with the so-called "war" on terror.

In violation of the Constitution, US law, the Geneva Conventions (to which the US is a signatory), and in violation of basic human rights, torture has been authorized by the President and his administration as official policy. Water-boarding, beatings, faked executions, confinement in extreme cold or extreme heat, prolonged enforcement of painful stress positions, sleep deprivation, sexual humiliation, and the defiling of religious articles have been practiced and exposed as routine at Guantanamo, at Abu Ghraib Prison and other US detention sites in Iraq, and at Bagram Air Base in Afghanistan. The president, besides bearing responsibility for authorizing the use of torture, also as Commander in Chief, bears ultimate responsibility for the failure to halt these practices and to punish those responsible once they were exposed.

The administration has sought to claim the abuse of captives is not torture, by redefining torture. An August 1, 2002 memorandum from the Administration's Office of Legal Counsel Jay S. Bybee addressed to White House Counsel Alberto R. Gonzales concluded that to constitute torture, any pain inflicted must be akin to that accompanying "serious physical injury, such as organ failure, impairment of bodily function, or even death." The memorandum went on to state that even should an act constitute torture under that minimal definition, it might still be permissible if applied to "interrogations undertaken pursuant to the President's Commander-in-Chief powers." The memorandum further asserted that "necessity or self-defense could provide justifications that would eliminate any criminal liability."

This effort to redefine torture by calling certain practices simply "enhanced interrogation techniques" flies in the face of the Third Geneva Convention Relating to the Treatment of Prisoners of War, which states that "No physical or mental torture, nor any other form of coercion, may be inflicted on prisoners of war to secure from them information of any kind whatever. Prisoners of war who refuse to answer may not be threatened, insulted, or exposed to any unpleasant or disadvantageous treatment of any kind."

Torture is further prohibited by the Universal Declaration of Human Rights, the paramount international human rights statement adopted unanimously by the United Nations General Assembly, including the United States, in 1948. Torture and other cruel, inhuman or degrading treatment or punishment is also prohibited by international treaties ratified by the United States: the International Covenant on Civil and Political Rights (ICCPR) and the Convention Against Torture and Other Cruel Inhuman or Degrading Treatment or Punishment (CAT).

When the Congress, in the Defense Authorization Act of 2006, overwhelmingly passed a measure banning torture and sent it to the President's desk for signature, the President, who together with his vice president, had fought hard to block passage of the amendment, signed it, but then quietly appended a signing statement in which he pointedly asserted that as Commander-in-Chief, he was not bound to obey its strictures.

The administration's encouragement of and failure to prevent torture of American captives in the wars in Iraq and Afghanistan, and in the battle against terrorism, has undermined the rule of law in the US and in the US military, and has seriously damaged both the effort to combat global terrorism, and more broadly, America's image abroad. In his effort to hide torture by US military forces and the CIA, the president has defied Congress and has lied to the American people, repeatedly claiming that the US "does not torture."

In all of these actions and decisions in violation of US and International law, President George W. Bush has acted in a manner contrary to his trust as President and Commander in Chief, and subversive of constitutional government, to the prejudice of the cause of law and justice and to the manifest injury of the people of the United States. Wherefore, President George W. Bush, by such conduct, is guilty of an impeachable offense warranting removal from office.

Article XVIII notes

Under the doctrine of "command responsibility," commanders, all the way up the chain of command to the commander-in-chief, are criminally liable if they knew or should have known their subordinates would commit crimes and the commander did nothing to stop or prevent it. The Third Geneva Convention in article 126 (concerning prisoners of war) and the Fourth Geneva Convention in article 143 (concerning detained civilians) require the International Committee of the Red Cross to have access to all detainees and places of detention. Visits may only be prohibited for "reasons of imperative military necessity" and then only as "an exceptional and temporary measure." In September 2004, two senior Army generals testified before the Senate Armed Services Committee that the CIA kept dozens of prisoners off official rosters at Abu Ghraib and other prisons in Iraq in order to hide them from the International Committee of the Red Cross. Donald Rumsfeld said he ordered a man called "Triple X" be held in secret, based on a request from CIA Director George Tenet. A classified order, issued at the behest of Rumsfeld by the top military commander in Iraq, said, "Notification of the presence and or status of the detainee to the International Committee of the Red Cross, or any international or national aid organization, is prohibited pending further guidance."

The Washington Post reported the CIA had been hiding and interrogating inmates at a secret facility in Eastern Europe, in "black sites" in eight countries under a global network set up after the September 11, 2001 attacks. In December 2005, the United States said it would continue to deny the International Committee of the Red Cross access to "a very small, limited number" of prisoners who are held in secret around the world. Abd al-Hadi al-Iraqi was kept in CIA custody from fall 2006 until spring 2007. The CIA kept his detention a secret from the International Committee of the Red Cross.

U.S Army Field Manual 27-10, Section 501.

Geneva Convention Relative to the Treatment of Prisoners of War art., 126, Aug. 12, 1949, 6 UST. 3316, 3320.

Geneva Convention Relative to the Protection of Civilian Persons in Time of War, art. 143, August 12, 1949, 6 UST. 3516, 75 U.N.T.S. 287.

United Nations Convention Against Torture and Other Cruel, Inhuman or Degrading Treatment or Punishment, opened for signature December 10, 1984, G.A. Res. 39/46, 39 U.N. GAOR Supp. No. 51, at 197, U.N. Doc. A/RES/39/708 (1984), entered into force June 26, 1987, 1465 U.N.T.S. 85, 23 I.L.M. 1027, (1984), as modified, 24 I.L.M. 535.

Foreign Affairs Reform and Restructuring Act of 1998, ("FARRA"), Pub. L. No. 105-277, § 2242, 112 Stat. 2681 (Oct. 21, 1998), reprinted in 8 USC. § 1231, Historical and Statutory Notes (1999).

International Covenant on Civil and Political Rights, G.A. Res. 2200A (XXI), U.N. GAOR, 21st Sess., Supp. No. 16, at 52, U.N. Doc. A/6316 Dec. 16, 1966, entered into force 23 March 1976, 999 U.N.T.S. 171; Human Rights Committee, General Comment 31, Nature of the General Legal Obligation on States Parties to the Covenant, U.N. Doc. CCPR/C/21/Rev.1/Add.13 (2004) (HRC General Comment 31).

Article XIX

RENDITION: KIDNAPPING PEOPLE AND TAKING THEM AGAINST THEIR WILL TO "BLACK SITES" LOCATED IN OTHER NATIONS, INCLUDING NATIONS KNOWN TO PRACTICE TORTURE

In his conduct while President of the United States, George W. Bush, in violation of his constitutional oath to faithfully execute the office of President of the United States and, to the best of his ability, preserve, protect, and defend the Constitution of the United States, and in violation of his constitutional duty under Article II, Section 3 of the Constitution "to take care that the laws be faithfully executed," has both personally and acting through his agents and subordinates, together with the Vice President, violated United States and International Law and the US Constitution by kidnapping people and renditioning them to "black sites" located in other nations, including nations known to practice torture.

The president has publicly admitted that since the 9-11 attacks in 2001, the US has been kidnapping and transporting against the will of the subject (renditioning) in its so-called "war" on terror—even people captured by US personnel in friendly nations like Sweden, Germany, Macedonia and Italy—and ferrying them to places like Bagram Airbase in Afghanistan, and to prisons operated in Eastern European countries, African Countries and Middle Eastern countries where security forces are known to practice torture.

These people are captured and held indefinitely, without any charges being filed, and are held without being identified to the Red Cross, or to their families. Many are clearly innocent, and several cases, including one in Canada and one in Germany, have demonstrably been shown subsequently to have been in error, because of a similarity of names or because of misinformation provided to US authorities.

Such a policy is in clear violation of US and International Law, and has placed the United States in the position of a pariah state. The CIA has no law enforcement authority, and cannot legally arrest or detain anyone. The program of "extraordinary rendition" authorized by the president is the substantial equivalent of the policies of "disappearing" people, practices widely practiced and universally condemned in the military dictatorships of Latin America during the late 20th Century.

The administration has claimed that prior administrations have practiced extraordinary rendition, but, while this is technically true, earlier renditions were used only to capture people with outstanding arrest warrants or convictions who were outside in order to deliver them to stand trial or serve their sentences in the US. The president has refused to divulge how many people have been subject to extraordinary rendition since September, 2001. It is possible that some have died in captivity. As one US official has stated off the record, regarding the program, Some of those who were renditioned were later delivered to Guantanamo, while others were sent there directly. An example of this is the case of six Algerian Bosnians who, immediately after being cleared by the Supreme Court of Bosnia Herzegovina in January 2002 of allegedly plotting to attack the US and UK embassies, were captured, bound and gagged by US special forces and renditioned to Guantanamo.

In perhaps the most egregious proven case of rendition, Maher Arar, a Canadian citizen born in Syria, was picked up in September 2002 while transiting through New York's JFK airport on his way home to Canada. Immigration and FBI officials detained and interrogated him for nearly two weeks, illegally denying him his rights to access counsel, the Canadian consulate, and the courts. Executive branch officials asked him if he would volunteer to go to Syria, where he hadn't been in 15 years, and Maher refused.

Maher was put on a private jet plane operated by the CIA and sent to Jordan, where he was beaten for 8 hours, and then delivered to Syria, where he was beaten and interrogated for 18 hours a day for a couple of weeks. He was whipped on his back and hands with a 2-inch thick electric cable and asked questions similar to those he had been asked in the United States. For over ten months Maher was held in an underground grave-like cell—3 x 6 x 7 feet—which was damp and cold, and in which the only light came in through a hole in the ceiling. After a year of this, Maher was released without any charges. He is now back home in Canada with his family. Upon his release, the Syrian Government announced he had no links to Al Qaeda, and the Canadian Government has also said they've found no links to Al

Qaeda. The Canadian Government launched a Commission of Inquiry into the Actions of Canadian Officials in Relation to Maher Arar, to investigate the role of Canadian officials, but the Bush Administration has refused to cooperate with the Inquiry.

Hundreds of flights of CIA-chartered planes have been documented as having passed through European countries on extraordinary rendition missions like that involving Maher Arar, but the administration refuses to state how many people have been subjects of this illegal program.

The same US laws prohibiting aiding and abetting torture also prohibit sending someone to a country where there is a substantial likelihood they may be tortured. Article 3 of CAT prohibits forced return where there is a "substantial likelihood" that an individual "may be in danger of" torture, and has been implemented by federal statute. Article 7 of the ICCPR prohibits return to country of origin where individuals may be "at risk" of either torture or cruel, inhuman or degrading treatment.

Under international Human Rights law, transferring a POW to any nation where he or she is likely to be tortured or inhumanely treated violates Article 12 of the Third Geneva Convention, and transferring any civilian who is a protected person under the Fourth Geneva Convention is a grave breach and a criminal act.

In situations of armed conflict, both international human rights law and humanitarian law apply. A person captured in the zone of military hostilities "must have some status under international law; he is either a prisoner of war and, as such, covered by the Third Convention, [or] a civilian covered by the Fourth Convention. There is no intermediate status; nobody in enemy hands can be outside the law." Although the state is obligated to repatriate Prisoners of War as soon as hostilities cease, the ICRC's commentary on the 1949 Conventions states that prisoners should not be repatriated where there are serious reasons for fearing that repatriating the individual would be contrary to general principles of established international law for the protection of human beings. Thus, all of the Guantánamo detainees as well as renditioned captives are protected by international human rights protections and humanitarian law.

By his actions as outlined above, the President has abused his power, broken the law, deceived the American people, and placed American military personnel, and indeed all Americans—especially those who may travel or live abroad--at risk of similar treatment. Furthermore, in the eyes of the rest of the world, the President has made the US, once a model of respect for Human Rights and respect for the rule of law, into a state where international law is neither respected nor upheld.

In all of these actions and decisions in violation of United States and International law, President George W. Bush has acted in a manner contrary to his trust as President and Commander in Chief, and subversive of constitutional government, to the prejudice of the cause of law and justice and to the manifest injury of the people of the United States. Wherefore, President George W. Bush, by such conduct, is guilty of an impeachable offense warranting removal from office.

Article XIX notes

Eric Schmitt and Douglas Jehl, "Army Says CIA Hid More Iraqis Than It Claimed," *New York Times*, September 10, 2004. http://www.nytimes.com/2004/09/10/politics/10abuse.html

Edward T. Pound, "Iraq's invisible man: A 'Ghost' Inmate's Strange Life Behind Bars, *US News & World Report*, June 20, 2004. http://www.usnews.com/usnews/news/articles/040628/28prison.htm

Dana Priest, "CIA Holds Terror Suspects in Secret Prisons: Debate Is Growing Within Agency About Legality and Morality of Overseas System Set Up After 9/11," *Washington Post*, November 2, 2005. http://www.washingtonpost.com/wp-dyn/content/article/2005/11/01/AR2005110101644.html

Mark Benjamin, "The CIA's latest 'ghost detainee': New details confirm a CIA prisoner disappeared in US Custody for Months, Renewing Suspicions the Agency Could be Violating the Law and Using Torture, *Salon*, May 22, 2007. http://www.salon.com/news/feature/2007/05/22/cia_prisoner

Syria: Country Reports on Human Rights Practices, Continuing Serious Abuses Including the Use of Torture in Detention, Which at Times Resulted in Death, 2004. http://www.state.gov/g/drl/rls/hrrpt/2004/41732.htm

IACHR, Report on Terrorism and Human Rights, OEA/Ser.L/V/II.1 16 Doc. 5 rev. 1 corr. (22 October 2002), at p.53 ¶ 61; IACHR, Third Report on the Situation of Human Rights in Colombia, OEA/Ser.L.V/II.102 doc. 9 rev. 1, 26 February 1999, at 95, Part IV, para. 83.

Article XX

IMPRISONING CHILDREN

In his conduct while President of the United States, George W. Bush, in violation of his constitutional oath to faithfully execute the office of President of the United States and, to the best of his ability, preserve, protect, and defend the Constitution of the United States, and in violation of his constitutional duty under Article II, Section 3 of the Constitution "to take care that the laws be faithfully executed," has both personally and acting through his agents and subordinates, authorized or permitted the arrest and detention of at least 2500 children under the age of 18 as "enemy combatants" in Iraq, Afghanistan, and at Guantanamo Bay Naval Station in violation of the Fourth Geneva Convention relating to the treatment of "protected persons" and the Optional Protocol to the Geneva Convention on the Rights of the Child on the Involvement of Children in Armed Conflict, signed by the US in 2002 . To wit:

In May 2008, the US government reported to the United Nations that it has been holding upwards of 2,500 children under the age of 18 as "enemy combatants" at detention centers in Iraq, Afghanistan and at Guantanamo Bay (where there was a special center, Camp Iguana, established just for holding children). The length of these detentions has frequently exceeded a year, and in some cases has stretched to five years. Some of these detainees have reached adulthood in detention and are now not being reported as child detainees because they are no longer children.

In addition to detaining children as "enemy combatants," it has been widely reported in media reports that the US military in Iraq has, based upon Pentagon rules of engagement, been treating boys as young as 14 years of age as "potential combatants," subject to arrest and even to being killed. In Fallujah, in the days ahead of the November 2004 all-out assault, Marines ringing the city were reported to be turning back into the city men and boys "of combat age" who were trying to flee the impending scene of battle—an act which in itself is a violation of the Geneva Conventions, which require combatants to permit anyone, combatants as well as civilians, to surrender, and to leave the scene of battle.

Under the Fourth Geneva Convention, to which the United States has been a signatory since 1949, children under the age of 15 captured in conflicts, even if they have been fighting, are to be considered victims, not prisoners. In 2002, the United States signed the Optional Protocol to the Geneva Convention on the Rights of the Child on the Involvement of children in Armed Conflict, which raised this age for this category of "protected person" to under 18.

The continued detention of such children, some as young as 10, by the US military is a violation of both convention and protocol, and as such constitutes a war crime for which the president, as commander in chief, bears full responsibility.

In all of these actions and decisions, President George W. Bush has acted in a manner contrary to his trust as President and Commander in Chief, and subversive of constitutional government, to the prejudice of the cause of law and justice and to the manifest injury of the people of the United States. Wherefore, President George W. Bush, by such conduct, is guilty of an impeachable offense warranting removal from office.

Article XX notes

Geneva Convention relative to the Protection of Civilian Persons in Time of War, Adopted on 12 August 1949 by the Diplomatic Conference for the Establishment of International Conventions for the Protection of Victims of War, held in Geneva, from 21 April to 12 August, 1949, entry into force 21 October 1950. http://www.unhchr.ch/html/menu3/b/92.htm

Optional Protocol to the Convention on the Rights of the Child on the involvement of children in armed conflict, Adopted and opened for signature, ratification and accession by General Assembly resolution, A/RES/54/263 of 25 May 2000, entered into force on 12 February 2002. http://www.unhchr.ch/html/menu2/6/protocolchild.htm

Severin Carrell, "The Children of Guantanamo Bay: The 'IoS' Reveals Today that More than 60 of the Detainees of the US camp Were Under 18 at the Time of their Capture, Some as Young as 14," The Independent, May 28, 2006. http://www.independent.co.uk/news/world/americas/the-children-of-guantanamo-bay-480059.html

Amnesty International, "Guantánamo: Pain and Distress for Thousands of Children November 20, 2006. http://www.amnesty.org/en/news-and-updates/feature-stories/guantanamo-pain-and-distress-for-thousands-of-children-20061120

Human Rights Watch, US: Guantanamo Kids at Risk, April 24, 2003. http://hrw.org/english/docs/2003/04/24/usint5782.htm

The Guardian, "US Detains Children at Guantanamo Bay," *The Guardian*, April 23, 2003. http://www.guardian.co.uk/world/2003/apr/23/usa

Human Rights Watch, "US: Despite Releases, Children Still Held at Guantanamo: Release of Three Children a Welcome Step, But Others Still Held," January 29, 2004. http://www.hrw.org/english/docs/2004/01/29/usint7117.htm

Clive Stafford Smith, "The Kids of Guantanamo Bay, June 15, 2005. http://www.cageprisoners.com/articles.php?id=7880

William Glaberson, "A Legal Debate in Guantánamo on Boy Fighters," *New York Times*, June 3, 2007. http://www.nytimes.com/2007/06/03/us/03gitmo.html?en=d65730e1824cbf0b&ex=1338523200&adxnnl=1&amp;amp;amp;ei=5124&partner=permalink&exprod=permalink&adxnnlx=1212845547-KbnVpkODE4618cLEfVKtrA

Associated Press, June 7, 2008, "UN decries war crimes charges against Gitmo minors."

Michelle Shephard, "UN committee criticizes US over trials: Prosecution and Detention of Child Soldiers in Iraq and Afghanistan 'Should be Prevented,' Report Says," *Toronto Star*, June 7, 2008. http://www.thestar.com/News/World/article/439093

Article XXI

MISLEADING CONGRESS AND THE AMERICAN PEOPLE ABOUT THREATS FROM IRAN, AND SUPPORTING TERRORIST ORGANIZATIONS WITHIN IRAN, WITH THE GOAL OF OVERTHROWING THE IRANIAN GOVERNMENT

In his conduct while President of the United States, George W. Bush, in violation of his constitutional oath to faithfully execute the office of President of the United States and, to the best of his ability, preserve, protect, and defend the Constitution of the United States, and in violation of his constitutional duty to take care that the laws be faithfully executed, has both personally and acting through his agents and subordinates misled the Congress and the citizens of the United States about a threat of nuclear attack from the nation of Iran.

The National Intelligence Estimate released to Congress and the public on December 4, 2007, which confirmed that the government of the nation of Iran had ceased any efforts to develop nuclear weapons, was completed in 2006. Yet , the president and his aides continued to suggest during 2007 that such a nuclear threat was developing and might already exist. National Security Adviser Stephen Hadley stated at the time the National Intelligence Estimate regarding Iran was released that the president had been briefed on its findings "in the last few months." Hadley's statement establishes a timeline that shows the president knowingly sought to deceive Congress and the American people about a nuclear threat that did not exist.

Hadley has stated that the president "was basically told: stand down" and, yet, the president and his aides continued to make false claims about the prospect that Iran was trying to "build a nuclear weapon" that could lead to "World War III."

This evidence establishes that the president actively engaged in and had full knowledge of a campaign by his administration to make a false "case" for an attack on Iran, thus warping the national security debate at a critical juncture and creating the prospect of an illegal and unnecessary attack on a sovereign nation.

Even after the National Intelligence Estimate was released to Congress and the American people, the president stated that he did not believe anything had changed and suggested that he and members of his administration would continue to argue that Iran should be seen as posing a threat to the United States. He did this despite the fact that United States intelligence agencies had clearly and officially stated that this was not the case.

Evidence suggests that the Bush Administration's attempts to portray Iran as a threat are part of a broader US policy toward Iran. On September 30, 2001, then-Secretary of Defense Donald Rumsfeld established an official military objective of overturning the regime in Iran, as well as those in Iraq, Syria, and four other countries in the Middle East, according to a document quoted in then-Undersecretary of Defense for Policy Douglas Feith's book, *War and Decision*.

General Wesley Clark, reports in his book *Winning Modern Wars* being told by a friend in the Pentagon in November 2001 that the list of governments that Rumsfeld and Deputy Secretary of Defense Paul Wolfowitz planned to overthrow included Iraq, Iran, Syria, Libya, Sudan, and Somalia. Clark writes that the list also included Lebanon.

Journalist Gareth Porter reported in May 2008 asking Feith at a public event which of the six regimes on the Clark list were included in the Rumsfeld paper, to which Feith replied, "All of them."

Rumsfeld's aides also drafted a second version of the paper, as instructions to all military commanders in the development of "campaign plans against terrorism". The paper called for military commanders to assist other government agencies "as directed" to "encourage populations dominated by terrorist organizations or their supporters to overthrow that domination."

In January 2005, Seymour Hersh reported in the *New Yorker* magazine that the Bush Administration had been conducting secret reconnaissance missions inside Iran at least since the summer of 2004.

In June 2005 former United Nations weapons inspector Scott Ritter reported that United States security forces had been sending members of the Mujahedeen-e Khalq (MEK) into Iranian territory. The MEK has been designated a terrorist organization by the United States, the European Union, Canada, Iraq, and Iran. Ritter reported that the United States

Central Intelligence Agency (CIA) had used the MEK to carry out remote bombings in Iran.

In April 2006, Hersh reported in the New Yorker Magazine that US combat troops had entered and were operating in Iran, where they were working with minority groups including the Azeris, Baluchis, and Kurds.

Also in April 2006, Larisa Alexandrovna reported on Raw Story that the US Department of Defense (DOD) was working with and training the MEK, or former members of the MEK, sending them to commit acts of violence in southern Iran in areas where recent attacks had left many dead. Raw Story reported that the Pentagon had adopted the policy of supporting MEK shortly after the 2003 invasion of Iraq, and in response to the influence of Vice President Richard B. Cheney's office. Raw Story subsequently reported that no Presidential finding, and no Congressional oversight, existed on MEK operations.

In March 2007, Hersh reported in the *New Yorker* Magazine that the Bush administration was attempting to stem the growth of Shiite influence in the Middle East (specifically the Iranian government and Hezbollah in Lebanon) by funding violent Sunni organizations, without any Congressional authorization or oversight. Hersh said funds had been given to "three Sunni jihadist groups ... connected to al Qaeda" that "want to take on Hezbollah."

In April 2008, the *Los Angeles Times* reported that conflicts with insurgent groups along Iran's borders were understood by the Iranian government as a proxy war with the United States. Among the groups the US DOD is supporting, according to this report, is the Party for Free Life in Kurdistan, known by its Kurdish acronym, PEJAK. The United States has provided "foodstuffs, economic assistance, medical supplies and Russian military equipment, some of it funneled through nonprofit groups."

In May 2008, Andrew Cockburn reported on CounterPunch that President Bush, six weeks earlier had signed a secret finding authorizing a covert offensive against the Iranian regime. President Bush's secret directive covers actions across an area stretching from Lebanon to Afghanistan, and purports to sanction actions up to and including the funding of organizations like the MEK and the assassination of public officials.

All of these actions by the president and his agents and subordinates exhibit a disregard for the truth and a recklessness with regard to national security, nuclear proliferation and the global role of the United States military that is not merely unacceptable but dangerous in a commander-in-chief.

In all of these actions and decisions, President George W. Bush has acted in a manner contrary to his trust as President and Commander in Chief, and subversive of constitutional government, to the prejudice of the cause of law and justice and to the manifest injury of the people of the United States. Wherefore, President George W. Bush, by such conduct, is guilty of an impeachable offense warranting removal from office.

Article XXI notes

National Intelligence Estimate Key Judgments: Iran: Nuclear Intentions and Capabilities, December 12, 2007. http://www.dni.gov/press_releases/20071203_release.pdf

Press Briefing by National Security Advisor Stephen Hadley, December 3, 2007. http://www.whitehouse.gov/news/releases/2007/12/20071203-10.html

Press Conference by the President, December 4, 2007. http://www.whitehouse.gov/news/releases/2007/12/20071204-4.html

Jennifer Van Bergen, "Scholar says Bush has used obscure doctrine to extend power 95 times (Unitary Executive Theory)," *Raw Story*, September 23, 2005. http://rawstory.com/news/2005/CanExecutive_Branch_Decide_0923.html

Tom Head, "Civil Liberties," About.com. http://civilliberty.about.com/od/waronterror/p/imperial101.htm

Scott Ritter, "Target Iran," Democracy Now, October 16, 2006. http://www.democracynow.org/2006/10/16/scott_ritter_on_target_iran_the

Robert Dreyfuss, "Shirin Ebadi: Don't Attack Iran," The Nation," April 29, 2008. http://www.thenation.com/doc/20080512/dreyfuss".

Prof. Marjorie Cohn, "Beware Attack on Iran," Global Research, March 17, 2008. http://www.globalresearch.ca/index.php?context=va&aid=8371

Documentation of Iran propaganda Campaign. http://democrats.com/iran-war-lies

Gareth Porter, "Pentagon Targeted Iran for Regime Change after 9/11," IPS. http://afterdowningstreet.org/node/33238

Seymour M. Hersh, "The Iran Plans: Would President Bush Go to War to Stop Tehran From Getting the Bomb?," *The New Yorker*, April 17, 2006. http://www.newyorker.com/archive/2006/04/17/060417fa_fact

Larisa Alexandrovna, "On Cheney, Rumsfeld Order, US Outsourcing Special Ops, Intelligence to Iraq Terror Group, Intelligence Officials Say," *Raw Story*, April 13, 2006. http://www.rawstory.com/printstory.php?story=1840

Seymour M. Hersh, "The Redirection: Is the Administration's New Policy Benefiting our

Enemies in the War on Terrorism?," *The New Yorker*, March 5, 2007. http://www.newyorker.com/reporting/2007/03/05/070305fa_fact_hersh?printable=true

Borzou Daragahi, "Iran says US Aids Rebels at its Borders: The violence May be Driving Tehran's Efforts to Back its Own Allies in Iraq," *Los Angeles Times*, April 15, 2008. http://www.latimes.com/news/nationworld/world/la-fg-proxy15apr15,1,6136619.story

Andrew Cockburn, "Secret Bush 'Finding' Widens War on Iran," *Counter Punch*, May 2, 2008. http://www.counterpunch.org/andrew05022008.html

Article XXII

CREATING SECRET LAWS

In his conduct while President of the United States, George W. Bush, in violation of his constitutional oath to faithfully execute the office of President of the United States and, to the best of his ability, preserve, protect, and defend the Constitution of the United States, and in violation of his constitutional duty under Article II, Section 3 of the Constitution "to take care that the laws be faithfully executed," has both personally and acting through his agents and subordinates, together with the Vice President, established a body of secret laws through the issuance of legal opinions by the Department of Justice's Office of Legal Counsel (OLC).

The OLC's March 14, 2003, interrogation memorandum ("Yoo Memorandum") was declassified years after it served as law for the executive branch. On April 29, 2008, House Judiciary Committee Chairman John Conyers and Subcommittee on the Constitution, Civil Rights and Civil Liberties Chairman Jerrold Nadler wrote in a letter to Attorney General Michael Mukasey:

"It appears to us that there was never any legitimate basis for the purely legal analysis contained in this document to be classified in the first place. The Yoo Memorandum does not describe sources and methods of intelligence gathering, or any specific facts regarding any interrogation activities. Instead, it consists almost entirely of the Department's legal views, which are not properly kept secret from Congress and the American people. J. William Leonard, the Director of the National Archive's Office of Information Security Oversight Office, and a top expert in this field concurs, commenting that '[t]he document in question is purely a legal analysis' that contains 'nothing which would justify classification.' In addition, the Yoo Memorandum suggests an extraordinary breadth and aggressiveness of OLC's secret legal opinion-making. Much attention has rightly been given to the statement in footnote 10 in the March 14, 2003, memorandum that, in an October 23, 2001, opinion, OLC concluded 'that the Fourth Amendment had no application to domestic military operations.' As you know, we have requested a copy of that memorandum on no less than four prior occasions and we continue to demand access to this important document.

"In addition to this opinion, however, the Yoo Memorandum references at least 10 other OLC opinions on weighty matters of great interest to the American people that also do not appear to have been released. These appear to cover matters such as the power of Congress to regulate the conduct of military commissions, legal constraints on the 'military detention of United States citizens,' legal rules applicable to the boarding and searching foreign ships, the President's authority to render US detainees to the custody of foreign governments, and the President's authority to breach or suspend US treaty obligations. Furthermore, it has been more than five years since the Yoo Memorandum was authored, raising the question how many other such memoranda and letters have been secretly authored and utilized by the Administration.

"Indeed, a recent court filing by the Department in FOIA litigation involving the Central Intelligence Agency identifies 8 additional secret OLC opinions, dating from August 6, 2004, to February 18, 2007. Given that these reflect only OLC memoranda identified in the files of the CIA, and based on the sampling procedures under which that listing was generated, it appears that these represent only a small portion of the secret OLC memoranda generated during this time, with the true number almost certainly much higher."

Senator Russ Feingold, in a statement during an April 30, 2008, Senate hearing stated:

"It is a basic tenet of democracy that the people have a right to know the law. In keeping with this principle, the laws passed by Congress and the case law of our courts have historically been matters of public record. And when it became apparent in the middle of the 20th century that federal agencies were increasingly creating a body of non-public administrative law, Congress passed several statutes requiring this law to be made public, for the express purpose of preventing a regime of 'secret law.'" That purpose today is being thwarted. Congressional enactments and agency regulations are for the most part still public. But the law that applies in this country is determined not only by statutes and regulations, but also by the controlling interpretations of courts and, in some cases, the executive branch. More and more, this body of executive and judicial law is being kept secret from the public, and too often from Congress as well....

"A legal interpretation by the Justice Department's Office of Legal Counsel ... binds the entire executive branch, just like a regulation or the ruling of a court. In the words of former OLC head Jack Goldsmith, 'These executive branch precedents are "law" for the executive branch.' The Yoo memorandum was, for a nine-month period in 2003 until it was withdrawn by Mr. Goldsmith, the law that this Administration followed when it came to matters of torture. And of course, that law was essentially a declaration that few if any laws applied...

"Another body of secret law is the controlling interpretations of the Foreign Intelligence Surveillance Act that are issued by the Foreign Intelligence Surveillance Court. FISA, of course, is the law that governs the government's ability in intelligence investigations to conduct wiretaps and search the homes of people in the United States. Under that statute, the FISA Court is directed to evaluate wiretap and search warrant applications and decide whether the standard for issuing a warrant has been met – a largely factual evaluation that is properly done behind closed doors. But with the evolution of technology and with this Administration's efforts to get the Court's blessing for its illegal wiretapping activities, we now know that the Court's role is broader, and that it is very much engaged in substantive interpretations of the governing statute. These interpretations are as much a part of this country's surveillance law as the statute itself. Without access to them, it is impossible for Congress or the public to have an informed debate on matters that deeply affect the privacy and civil liberties of all Americans...

"The Administration's shroud of secrecy extends to agency rules and executive pronouncements, such as Executive Orders, that carry the force of law. Through the diligent efforts of my colleague Senator Whitehouse, we have learned that OLC has taken the position that a President can 'waive' or 'modify' a published Executive Order without any notice to the public or Congress—simply by not following it."

In all of these actions and decisions, President George W. Bush has acted in a manner contrary to his trust as President, and subversive of constitutional government, to the prejudice of the cause of law and justice and to the manifest injury of the people of the United States. Wherefore, President George W. Bush, by such conduct, is guilty of an impeachable offense warranting removal from office.

Article XXII notes

Letter from Congressmen John Conyers and Jerrold Nadler to Attorney General Michael Mukasey, April 29, 2008. http://afterdowningstreet.org/node/33120

Statement of Senator Russ Feingold, April 30, 2008. http://judiciary.senate.gov/member_statement. cfm?id=3305&wit_id=4083

Hearing before the Senate Committee on the Judiciary Subcommittee on the Constitution on Secret Law and the Threat to Democratic and Accountable Government, Wednesday, April 30, 2008. http:// judiciary.senate.gov/hearing.cfm?id=3305

John C. Yoo, Memorandum for William J. Haynes II, Re: Military Interrogation of Alien Unlawful Combatants Held Outside the United States, March 14, 2003. http://www.aclu.org/pdfs/safefree/yoo_army_ torture_memo.pdf

John Conyers, Jr., Letter to Professor John Choo Yoo — Requests Testimony, April 8, 2008. http://tpm-muckraker.talkingpointsmemo.com/2008/04/conyers_schedules_hearing_with.php

Electronic Privacy Information Center v. United States Department of Justice, Civil Action No. 06-0096 (HHK), April 3, 2008.

American Civil Liberties Union et al v. United States Department of Justice, Civil Action No. 06-00214 (HHK), April 3, 2008. http://www.aclu.org/images/nsaspying/asset_upload_file985_34833.pdf

Article XXIII

VIOLATION OF THE POSSE COMITATUS ACT

In his conduct while President of the United States, George W. Bush, in violation of his constitutional oath to faithfully execute the office of President of the United States and, to the best of his ability, preserve, protect, and defend the Constitution of the United States, and in violation of his constitutional duty under Article II, Section 3 of the Constitution "to take care that the laws be faithfully executed," has both personally and acting through his agents and subordinates, repeatedly and illegally established programs to appropriate the power of the military for use in law enforcement. Specifically, he has contravened USC. Title 18. Section 1385, originally enacted in 1878, subsequently amended as "Use of Army and Air Force as Posse Comitatus" and commonly known as the Posse Comitatus Act.

The Act states:

"Whoever, except in cases and under circumstances expressly authorized by the Constitution or Act of Congress, willfully uses any part of the Army or the Air Force as a posse comitatus or otherwise to execute the laws shall be fined under this title or imprisoned not more than two years, or both."

The Posse Comitatus Act is designed to prevent the military from becoming a national police force.

The Declaration of Independence states as a specific grievance against the British that the King had "kept among us, in times of peace, Standing Armies without the consent of our legislatures," had "affected to render the Military independent of and superior to the civil power," and had "quarter[ed] large bodies of armed troops among us . . . protecting them, by a mock trial, from punishment for any murders which they should commit on the inhabitants of these States"

Despite the Posse Comitatus Act's intent, and in contravention of the law, President Bush:

a) has used military forces for law enforcement purposes on US border patrol;

b) has established a program to use military personnel for surveillance and information on criminal activities;

c) is using military espionage equipment to collect intelligence information for law enforcement use on civilians within the United States; and

d) employs active duty military personnel in surveillance agencies, including the Central Intelligence Agency (CIA).

In June 2006, President Bush ordered National Guard troops deployed to the border shared by Mexico with Arizona, Texas, and California. This deployment, which by 2007 reached a maximum of 6,000 troops, had orders to "conduct surveillance and operate detection equipment, work with border entry identification teams, analyze information, assist with communications and give administrative support to the Border Patrol" and concerned "… providing intelligence…inspecting cargo, and conducting surveillance."

The Air Force's "Eagle Eyes" program encourages Air Force military staff to gather evidence on American citizens. Eagle Eyes instructs Air Force personnel to engage in surveillance and then advises them to "alert local authorities," asking military staff to surveil and gather evidence on public citizens. This contravenes DoD Directive 5525.5 "SUBJECT: DoD Cooperation with Civilian Law Enforcement" which limits such activities.

President Bush has implemented a program to use imagery from military satellites for domestic law enforcement through the National Applications Office.

President Bush has assigned numerous active duty military personnel to civilian institutions such as the CIA and the Department of Homeland Security, both of which have responsibilities for law enforcement and intelligence.

In addition, on May 9, 2007, President Bush released "National Security Presidential Directive/NSPD 51," which effectively gives the president unchecked power to control the entire government and to define that government in time of an emergency, as well as the power to determine whether there is an emergency. The document also contains "classified Continuity Annexes." In July 2007 and again in August 2007 Rep. Peter DeFazio, a senior member of the House Homeland Security Committee, sought access to the classified annexes. DeFazio and other leaders of the Homeland Security Committee, including Chairman Bennie Thompson, have been denied a review of the Continuity of Government classified annexes.

In all of these actions and decisions, President George W. Bush has acted in a manner contrary to his trust as President, and subversive of constitutional government, to the prejudice of the cause of law and justice and to the manifest injury of the people of the United States. Wherefore, President George W. Bush, by such conduct, is guilty of an impeachable offense warranting removal from office.

Article XXIII notes

Charles Doyle, "The Posse Comitatus Act and Related Matters: The Use of the Military to Execute Civilian Law." CRS Report for Congress. Updated June 1, 2000.

Gerry J. Gilmore, Guard Plans to Adjust Number of Troops Serving on US-Mexican Border, American Forces Press Services. US National Guard Web Site, July 12, 2007. http://www.ngb.army.mil/news/archives/2007/07/071207-Border_troops.aspx

Diedtra Henderson, "Skepticism Voiced on Role of Troops," Boston Globe, May 15, 2006. http://www.boston.com/news/nation/articles/2006/05/15/putting_guard_on_border_debated

Tech Sgt. John Jung, Holiday Season Eagle Eyes, Air Force Office of Special Investigations Web Site, November 8, 2007. http://www.osi.andrews.af.mil/news/story.asp?id=123075173

According to the "Holiday Season Eagle Eyes" website, among the items Air Force Personnel are advised to look for are: "… people who don't seem to belong in the neighborhood, business establishment, or anywhere else. This category is hard to define, but the point is that people know what looks right and what doesn't look right in their neighborhoods, stores, malls etc., and if a person just doesn't seem like he or she belongs, there's probably a reason for that." Once identified, then the individual may be reported to "local authorities."

US Department of Defense. DoD Directive 5525.5 SUBJECT: DoD. Cooperation with Civilian Law Enforcement. E4.1.3. Restrictions on Direct Assistance. This directive "regards the prohibition on the use of military personnel 'as a posse comitatus or otherwise to execute the laws' [and] prohibits the following forms of direct assistance: E4.1.3.4. Use of military personnel for surveillance or pursuit of individuals, or as undercover agents, informants, investigators, or interrogators.

According to the NAO Fact Sheet:"The US Department of Homeland Security's (DHS) National Applications Office (NAO) is the executive agent to facilitate the use of intelligence community technological assets for civil, homeland security and law enforcement purposes within the United States." US Department of Homeland Security Fact Sheet /a : National Applications Office, Release Date August 15, 2007. http://www.dhs.gov/xnews/releases/pr_1187188414685.shtm

Organizations that would contribute to such activities include the National Reconnaissance Office (NRO), which develops and operates satellites, and the National Geospatial-Intelligence Agency (NGA) which provides GPS products and analyzes GPS data. Both of these NGA and NRO are agencies of the Department of Defense.

Article XXIV

SPYING ON AMERICAN CITIZENS, WITHOUT A COURT-ORDERED WARRANT, IN VIOLATION OF THE LAW AND THE FOURTH AMENDMENT

In his conduct while President of the United States, George W. Bush, in violation of his constitutional oath to faithfully execute the office of President of the United States and, to the best of his ability, preserve, protect, and defend the Constitution of the United States, and in violation of his constitutional duty under Article II, Section 3 of the Constitution "to take care that the laws be faithfully executed," has both personally and acting through his agents and subordinates, knowingly violated the fourth Amendment to the Constitution and the Foreign Intelligence Service Act of 1978 (FISA) by authorizing warrantless electronic surveillance of American citizens to wit:

(1) The President was aware of the FISA Law requiring a court order for any wiretap as evidenced by the following:

(A) "Now, by the way, any time you hear the United States government talking about wiretap, it requires—a wiretap requires a court order. Nothing has changed, by the way. When we're talking about chasing down terrorists, we're talking about getting a court order before we do so." —White House Press conference on April 20, 2004 [White House Transcript]

(B) "Law enforcement officers need a federal judge's permission to wiretap a foreign terrorist's phone, or to track his calls, or to search his property. Officers must meet strict standards to use any of the tools we're talking about." —President Bush's speech in Baltimore Maryland on July 20th 2005 [White House Transcript]

(2) The President repeatedly ordered the NSA to place wiretaps on American citizens without requesting a warrant from FISA as evidenced by the following:

(A) "Months after the Sept. 11 attacks, President Bush secretly authorized the National Security Agency to eavesdrop on Americans and others inside the United States to search for evidence of terrorist activity without the court-approved warrants ordinarily required for domestic spying, according to government officials." —*New York Times* article by James Risen and Eric Lichtblau on December 12, 2005. [NYTimes]

(B) The President admits to authorizing the program by stating "I have reauthorized this program more than 30 times since the September the 11th attacks, and I intend to do so for as long as our nation faces a continuing threat from al Qaeda and related groups. The NSA's activities under this authorization are thoroughly reviewed by the Justice Department and NSA's top legal officials, including NSA's general counsel and inspector general. Leaders in Congress have been briefed more than a dozen times on this authorization and the activities conducted under it." —Radio Address from the White House on December 17, 2005 [White House Transcript]

(C) In a December 19th 2005 press conference the President publicly admitted to using a combination of surveillance techniques including some with permission from the FISA courts and some without permission from FISA.

Reporter: "It was, why did you skip the basic safeguards of asking courts for permission for the intercepts?"

THE PRESIDENT: ... We use FISA still -- you're referring to the FISA court in your question -- of course, we use FISAs. But FISA is for long-term monitoring. What is needed in order to protect the American people is the ability to move quickly to detect. Now, having suggested this idea, I then, obviously, went to the question, is it legal to do so? I am—I swore to uphold the laws. Do I have the legal authority to do this? And the answer is, absolutely. As I mentioned in my remarks, the legal authority is derived from the Constitution, as well as the authorization of force by the United States Congress." [White House Transcript]

(D) Mike McConnel, the Director of National Intelligence, in a letter to to Senator Arlen Specter, acknowledged that Bush's Executive Order in 2001 authorized a series of secret surveillance activities and included undisclosed activities beyond the warrantless surveillance of e-mails and phone calls that Bush confirmed in December 2005. —"NSA Spying Part of Broader Effort" by Dan Eggen, *Washington Post*, 8/1/07

(3) The President ordered the surveillance to be conducted in a way that would spy upon private communications between American citizens located within the United States borders as evidenced by the following:

(A) Mark Klein, a retired AT&T communications technician, submitted an affidavit in support of the Electronic Frontier Foundation's EFF's lawsuit against AT&T. He testified that in 2003 he connected a "splitter" that sent a copy of Internet traffic and phone calls to a secure room that was operated by the NSA in the San Francisco office of AT&T. He heard from a co-worker that similar rooms were being constructed in other cities, including Seattle, San Jose, Los Angeles and San Diego. —From "Whistle-Blower Outs NSA Spy Room," Wired News, 4/7/06 [Wired] [EFF Case]

(4) The President asserted an inherent authority to conduct electronic surveillance based on the Constitution and the "Authorization to use Military Force in Iraq" (AUMF) that was not legally valid as evidenced by the following:

(A) In a December 19th, 2005 Press Briefing General Alberto Gonzales admitted that the surveillance authorized by the President was not only done without FISA warrants, but that the nature of the surveillance was so far removed from what FISA can approve that FISA could not even be amended to allow it. Gonzales stated "We have had discussions with Congress in the past—certain members of Congress—as to whether or not FISA could be amended to allow us to adequately deal with this kind of threat, and we were advised that that would be difficult, if not impossible."

(B) The Fourth Amendment to the United States Constitution states "The right of the people to be secure in their persons, houses, papers, and effects, against unreasonable searches and seizures, shall not be violated, and no Warrants shall issue, but upon probable cause, supported by Oath or affirmation, and particularly describing the place to be searched, and the persons or things to be seized."

(C) "The Foreign Intelligence Surveillance Act of 1978 unambiguously limits warrantless domestic electronic surveillance, even in a congressionally declared war, to the first 15 days of that war; criminalizes any such electronic surveillance not authorized by statute; and expressly establishes FISA and two chapters of the federal criminal code, governing wiretaps for intelligence purposes and for criminal investigation, respectively, as the "exclusive means by which electronic surveillance . . . and the interception of domestic wire, oral, and electronic communications may be conducted." 50 USC. §§ 1811, 1809, 18 USC. § 2511(2)(f)." —Letter from Harvard Law Professor Lawrence Tribe to John Conyers on 1/6/06

(D) In a December 19th, 2005 Press Briefing Attorney General Alberto

Gonzales stated "Our position is, is that the authorization to use force, which was passed by the Congress in the days following September 11th, constitutes that other authorization, that other statute by Congress, to engage in this kind of signals intelligence."

(E) The "Authorization to use Military Force in Iraq" does not give any explicit authorization related to electronic surveillance. [HJRes114]

(F) "From the foregoing analysis, it appears unlikely that a court would hold that Congress has expressly or impliedly authorized the NSA electronic surveillance operations here under discussion, and it would likewise appear that, to the extent that those surveillances fall within the definition of 'electronic surveillance' within the meaning of FISA or any activity regulated under Title III, Congress intended to cover the entire field with these statutes." —From the "Presidential Authority to Conduct Warrantless Electronic Surveillance to Gather Foreign Intelligence Information" by the Congressional Research Service on January 5, 2006.

(G) "The inescapable conclusion is that the AUMF did not implicitly authorize what the FISA expressly prohibited. It follows that the presidential program of surveillance at issue here is a violation of the separation of powers — as grave an abuse of executive authority as I can recall ever having studied." —Letter from Harvard Law Professor Lawrence Tribe to John Conyers on 1/6/06

(H) On August 17, 2006 Judge Anna Diggs Taylor of the United States District Court in Detroit, in ACLU v. NSA, ruled that the "NSA program to wiretap the international communications of some Americans without a court warrant violated the Constitution. ... Judge Taylor ruled that the program violated both the Fourth Amendment and a 1978 law that requires warrants from a secret court for intelligence wiretaps involving people in the United States. She rejected the administration's repeated assertions that a 2001 Congressional authorization and the president's constitutional authority allowed the program." —From a *New York Times* article "Judge Finds Wiretap Actions Violate the Law" 8/18/06 and the Memorandum Opinion

(I) In July 2007, the Sixth Circuit Court of Appeals dismissed the case, ruling the plaintiffs had no standing to sue because, given the secretive nature of the surveillance, they could not state with certainty that they have been wiretapped by the NSA. This ruling did not address the legality of the surveillance so Judge Taylor's decision is the only ruling on that issue. [ACLU Legal Documents]

In all of these actions and decisions, President George W. Bush has acted in a manner contrary to his trust as President, and subversive of constitutional government, to the prejudice of the cause of law and justice and to the manifest injury of the people of the United States. Wherefore, President George W. Bush, by such conduct, is guilty of an impeachable offense warranting removal from office.

Article XXIV notes

White House Transcript, April 20, 2004. http://www.whitehouse.gov/news/releases/2004/04/20040420-2.html

White House Transcript, July 20, 2005. http://www.whitehouse.gov/news/releases/2005/07/20050720-4.html

James Risen and Eric Lichtblau, "Bush Secretly Lifted Some Limits on Spying in US After 9/11, Officials Say," New York Times, December 12, 2005. http://www.nytimes.com/2005/12/15/politics/15cnd-program.html"

White House Transcript, December 17, 2005. http://www.whitehouse.gov/news/releases/2005/12/20051217.html

White House Transcript, December 19, 2005. http://www.whitehouse.gov/news/releases/2005/12/20051219-2.html

Dan Eggen, "NSA Spying Part of Broader Effort," Washington Post, August 1, 2007. http://www.washingtonpost.com/wp-dyn/content/article/2007/07/31/AR2007073102137.html

Ryan Singel, "Whistle-Blower Outs NSA Spy Room," Wired, April 7, 2006. http://www.wired.com/science/discoveries/news/2006/04/70619

EFF's Class-Action Lawsuit Against AT&T for Collaboration with Illegal Domestic Spying Program. http://w2.eff.org/legal/cases/att

Alberto Gonzales Press Briefing, December 19, 2005. http://www.whitehouse.gov/news/releases/2005/12/print/200512191.html

Lawrence Tribe Letter, January 6, 2006. http://www.impeachbush.tv/archives/conyers_tribe_nsa_060106.pdf

HJ Res 114. http://thomas.loc.gov/cgi-bin/bdquery/z?d107:H.J.RES.114

Adam Liptak and Eric Lichtblau, "Judge Finds Wiretap Actions Violate the Law," New York Times, August 18, 2006. http://www.nytimes.com/2006/08/18/washington/18nsa.html

ACLU Legal Documents in Challenge to Illegal NSA Spying. http://www.aclu.org/safefree/nsaspying/26582res20060828.html

Article XXV

DIRECTING TELECOMMUNICATIONS COMPANIES TO CREATE AN ILLEGAL AND UNCONSTITUTIONAL DATABASE OF THE PRIVATE TELEPHONE NUMBERS AND EMAILS OF AMERICAN CITIZENS

In his conduct while President of the United States, George W. Bush, in violation of his constitutional oath to faithfully execute the office of President of the United States and, to the best of his ability, preserve, protect, and defend the Constitution of the United States, and in violation of his constitutional duty under Article II, Section 3 of the Constitution "to take care that the laws be faithfully executed," has both personally and acting through his agents and subordinates, violated the Stored Communications Act of 1986 and the Telecommunications Act of 1996 by creating of a very large database containing information related to the private telephone calls and emails of American citizens, to wit:

The President requested that telecommunication companies release customer phone records to the government illegally as evidenced by the following:

"The Stored Communications Act of 1986 (SCA) prohibits the knowing disclosure of customer telephone records to the government unless pursuant to subpoena, warrant or a National Security Letter (or other Administrative subpoena); with the customers lawful consent; or there is a business necessity; or an emergency involving the danger of death or serious physical injury. None of these exceptions apply to the circumstance described in the USA Today story."—From page 169, *George W Bush versus the US Constitution*. Compiled at the direction of Representative John Conyers.

According to a May 11, 2006 article in *USA Today* by Lesley Cauley, "The National Security Agency has been secretly collecting the phone call records of tens of millions of Americans, using data provided by AT&T, Verizon and Bell South." An unidentified source said 'The agency's goal is "to create a database of every call ever made" within the nation's borders."

In early 2001, Qwest CEO Joseph Nacchio rejected a request from the NSA to turn over customers records of phone calls, emails and other Internet activity. Nacchio believed that complying with the request would violate the Telecommunications Act of 1996. —From *National Journal*, November 2, 2007.

In all of these actions and decisions, President George W. Bush has acted in a manner contrary to his trust as President, and subversive of constitutional government, to the prejudice of the cause of law and justice and to the manifest injury of the people of the United States. Wherefore, President George W. Bush, by such conduct, is guilty of an impeachable offense warranting removal from office.

Article XXV notes

House Judiciary Committee Democratic Staff, George W. Bush vs. the US Constitution, 2005.

Telecommunications Act of 1996. http://www.fcc.gov/telecom.html

Shane Harris, "NSA Sought Data Before 9/11," *National Journal*, November 2, 2007. http://news.national-journal.com/articles/071102nj1.htm

"Telecoms May Face Trouble Over Phone Records," Seattle Times, May 13, 2006. http://seattletimes.nwsource.com/html/nationworld/2002991165_nsa13.html

Marguerite Reardon, "Verizon Sued for Alleged NSA Cooperation, CNET News.com, May 15, 2006. http://www.news.com/Verizon-sued-for-alleged-NSA-cooperation/2100-1036_3-6072483.html

Liz Pulliam Weston, "Who's Listening to Your Phone Calls?," MSN Money. http://articles.moneycentral.msn.com/Banking/FinancialPrivacy/Who'sListeningToYourPhoneCalls.aspx?page=all

US Code, Title 18, Part 1, Chapter 12 — Stored Wire and Electronic Communications and Transactional Records Access. 2701 — Unlawful access to stored communications, US Code Collection, Cornell University Law School. http://www.law.cornell.edu/uscode/18/usc_sec_18_00002701----000-.html

Leslie Cauley, "NSA has Massive Database of Americans' Phone Calls," *USA Today*, May 11, 2006. http://www.usatoday.com/news/washington/2006-05-10-nsa_x.htm

Article XXVI

ANNOUNCING THE INTENT TO VIOLATE LAWS WITH SIGNING STATEMENTS, AND VIOLATING THOSE LAWS

In his conduct while President of the United States, George W. Bush, in violation of his constitutional oath to faithfully execute the office of President of the United States and, to the best of his ability, preserve, protect, and defend the Constitution of the United States, and in violation of his constitutional duty under Article II, Section 3 of the Constitution "to take care that the laws be faithfully executed," has used signing statements to claim the right to violate acts of Congress even as he signs them into law.

In June 2007, the Government Accountability Office reported that in a sample of Bush signing statements the office had studied, for 30 percent of them the Bush administration had already proceeded to violate the laws the statements claimed the right to violate.

In all of these actions and decisions, President George W. Bush has acted in a manner contrary to his trust as President, and subversive of constitutional government, to the prejudice of the cause of law and justice and to the manifest injury of the people of the United States. Wherefore, President George W. Bush, by such conduct, is guilty of an impeachable offense warranting removal from office.

Article XXVI notes

GAO Report. http://rawstory.com/other/GAOLegalopinionB-308603.pdf

Charlie Savage, "Bush Challenges Hundreds of Laws: President Cites Powers of His Office, *The Boston Globe*, April 30, 2006. http://www.boston.com/news/nation/articles/2006/04/30/bush_challenges_hundreds_of_laws

Jennifer van Bergen, "The Unitary Executive: Is the Doctrine Behind the Bush Presidency Consistent with a Democratic State?," Findlaw: Legal News and Commentary, January 9, 2006. http://writ.news.findlaw.com/commentary/20060109_bergen.html

Article XXVI

Jonathan Weisman, "'Signing Statements' Study Finds Administration Has Ignored Laws," *Washington Post*, June 19, 2007, Page A04. http://www.washingtonpost.com/wp-dyn/content/article/2007/06/18/AR2007061801412.html

T. J. Halstead, "Presidential Signing Statements: Constitutional & Institutional Implications," CRS Report for Congress, Updated September 17, 2007. http://www.fas.org/sgp/crs/natsec/RL33667.pdf

United States Government Accountability Office, Presidential Signing Statements: Agency Implementation of Selected Provisions of Law, Washington, D.C, March 11, 2008. (GAO-08-553T). http://www.gao.gov/new.items/d08553t.pdf

Article XXVII

FAILING TO COMPLY WITH CONGRESSIONAL SUBPOENAS
AND INSTRUCTING FORMER EMPLOYEES NOT TO COMPLY

In his conduct while President of the United States, George W. Bush, in violation of his constitutional oath to faithfully execute the office of President of the United States and, to the best of his ability, preserve, protect, and defend the Constitution of the United States, and in violation of his constitutional duty under Article II, Section 3 of the Constitution "to take care that the laws be faithfully executed," has both personally and acting through his agents and subordinates, refused to comply with Congressional subpoenas, and instructed former employees not to comply with subpoenas.

Subpoenas not complied with include:

A House Judiciary Committee subpoena for Justice Department papers and Emails, issued April 10, 2007;

A House Oversight and Government Reform Committee subpoena for the testimony of the Secretary of State, issued April 25, 2007;

A House Judiciary Committee subpoena for the testimony of former White House Counsel Harriet Miers and documents , issued June 13, 2007;

A Senate Judiciary Committee subpoena for documents and testimony of White House Chief of Staff Joshua Bolten, issued June 13, 2007;

A Senate Judiciary Committee subpoena for documents and testimony of White House Political Director Sara Taylor, issued June 13, 2007 (Taylor appeared but refused to answer questions);

A Senate Judiciary Committee subpoena for documents and testimony of White House Deputy Chief of Staff Karl Rove, issued June 26, 2007;

A Senate Judiciary Committee subpoena for documents and testimony of White House Deputy Political Director J. Scott Jennings, issued June 26, 2007 (Jennings appeared but refused to answer questions);

A Senate Judiciary Committee subpoena for legal analysis and other documents concerning the NSA warrantless wiretapping program from the

White House, Vice President Richard Cheney, The Department of Justice, and the National Security Council. If the documents are not produced, the subpoena requires the testimony of White House chief of staff Josh Bolten, Attorney General Alberto Gonzales, Cheney chief of staff David Addington, National Security Council executive director V. Philip Lago, issued June 27, 2007;

A House Oversight and Government Reform Committee subpoena for Lt. General Kensinger.

In all of these actions and decisions, President George W. Bush has acted in a manner contrary to his trust as President, and subversive of constitutional government, to the prejudice of the cause of law and justice and to the manifest injury of the people of the United States. Wherefore, President George W. Bush, by such conduct, is guilty of an impeachable offense warranting removal from office.

Article XXVII notes

List of Bush Administration's many ignored subpoenas: http://democrats.com/subpoenas

Article XXVIII

TAMPERING WITH FREE AND FAIR ELECTIONS, CORRUPTION OF THE ADMINISTRATION OF JUSTICE,

In his conduct while President of the United States, George W. Bush, in violation of his constitutional oath to faithfully execute the office of President of the United States and, to the best of his ability, preserve, protect, and defend the Constitution of the United States, and in violation of his constitutional duty under Article II, Section 3 of the Constitution "to take care that the laws be faithfully executed," has both personally and acting through his agents and subordinates, conspired to undermine and tamper with the conduct of free and fair elections, and to corrupt the administration of justice by United States Attorneys and other employees of the Department of Justice, through abuse of the appointment power.

Toward this end, the President and Vice President, both personally and through their agents, did:

Engage in a program of manufacturing false allegations of voting fraud in targeted jurisdictions where the Democratic Party enjoyed an advantage in electoral performance or otherwise was problematic for the President's Republican Party, in order that public confidence in election results favorable to the Democratic Party be undermined;

Direct United States Attorneys to launch and announce investigations of certain leaders, candidates and elected officials affiliated with the Democratic Party at times calculated to cause the most political damage and confusion, most often in the weeks immediately preceding an election, in order that public confidence in the suitability for office of Democratic Party leaders, candidates and elected officials be undermined;

Direct United States Attorneys to terminate or scale back existing investigations of certain Republican Party leaders, candidates and elected officials allied with the George W. Bush administration, and to refuse to pursue new or proposed investigations of certain Republican Party leaders, candidates and elected officials allied with the George W. Bush administration, in order that public confidence in the suitability of such Republican Party leaders, candidates and elected officials be bolstered or restored;

Threaten to terminate the employment of the following United States Attorneys who refused to comply with such directives and purposes:

David C. Iglesias as US Attorney for the District of New Mexico;

Kevin V. Ryan as US Attorney for the Northern District of California;

John L. McKay as US Attorney for the Western District of Washington;

Paul K. Charlton as US Attorney for the District of Arizona;

Carol C. Lam as US Attorney for the Southern District of California;

Daniel G. Bogden as US Attorney for the District of Nevada;

Margaret M. Chiara as US Attorney for the Western District of Michigan;

Todd Graves as US Attorney for the Western District of Missouri;

Harry E. "Bud" Cummins, III as US Attorney for the Eastern District of Arkansas;

Thomas M. DiBiagio as US Attorney for the District of Maryland, and

Kasey Warner as US Attorney for the Southern District of West Virginia.

Further, George W. Bush has both personally and acting through his agents and subordinates, together with the Vice President conspired to obstruct the lawful Congressional investigation of these dismissals of United States Attorneys and the related scheme to undermine and tamper with the conduct of free and fair elections, and to corrupt the administration of justice.

Contrary to his oath faithfully to execute the office of President of the United States and, to the best of his ability, preserve, protect, and defend the Constitution of the United States, and in violation of his constitutional duty to take care that the laws be faithfully executed, George W. Bush has without lawful cause or excuse directed not to appear before the Committee on the Judiciary of the House of Representatives certain witnesses summoned by duly authorized subpoenas issued by that Committee on June 13, 2007.

In refusing to permit the testimony of these witnesses George W. Bush, substituting his judgment as to what testimony was necessary for the inquiry, interposed the powers of the Presidency against the lawful subpoenas of the House of Representatives, thereby assuming to himself functions and judgments necessary to the exercise of the checking and balancing power of oversight vested in the House of Representatives.

Further, the President has both personally and acting through his agents and subordinates, together with the Vice President directed the United States Attorney for the District of Columbia to decline to prosecute for contempt of Congress the aforementioned witnesses, Joshua B. Bolten and Harriet E. Miers, despite the obligation to do so as established by statute (2 USC § 194) and pursuant to the direction of the United States House of Representatives as embodied in its resolution (H. Res. 982) of February 14, 2008.

In all of these actions and decisions, President George W. Bush has acted in a manner contrary to his trust as President, and subversive of constitutional government, to the prejudice of the cause of law and justice and to the manifest injury of the people of the United States. Wherefore, President George W. Bush, by such conduct, is guilty of an impeachable offense warranting removal from office.

Article XXVIII notes

Dan Eggen and Amy Goldstein, "Voter-Fraud Complaints by GOP Drove Dismissals," *Washington Post*, May 14, 2007. http://www.washingtonpost.com/wp-dyn/content/article/2007/05/13/AR2007051301106.html

Rebecca Carr, "Former Justice Official: Fired US Attorneys Among the Best, Cox Newspapers, May 8, 2007. http://www.coxwashington.com/news/content/reporters/stories/2007/05/08/BC_FIRED_PROSECU-TORS04_COX.html

Marisa Taylor, "Gonzales Appoints Political Loyalists into Vacant US Attorneys Slots, McClatchy Newspapers, January 26, 2007. http://www.realcities.com/mld/krwashington/news/nation/16555903.htm

David Bowermaster, "Charges May Result From Firings, Say Two Former US Attorneys, *Seattle Times*, May 9, 2007. http://seattletimes.nwsource.com/html/localnews/2003699882_webmckayforum09m.html

Murray Waas, "Secret Order By Gonzales Delegated Extraordinary Powers To Aides," *National Journal*, National Journal Group, Inc., April 30, 2007. http://news.nationaljournal.com/articles/070430nj1.htm

David Stout, "Ex-Gonzales Aide Testifies, 'I Crossed the Line,'" *New York Times*, May 23, 2007. http://www.nytimes.com/2007/05/23/washington/23cnd-monica.html?_r=1&hp&oref=slogin

Richard Roesler, "No Evidence of Election Crime, Former US Attorney Says," *Spokesman Review*, May 20, 2007. http://www.spokesmanreview.com/breaking/story.asp?ID=9951

Jan Crawford Greenberg, "E-Mails Show Rove's Role in US Attorney Firings," ABC News, March 15, 2007. http://abcnews.go.com/Politics/story?id=2954988&page=1

Dan Eggen, "Firings Had Genesis in White House Ex-Counsel Miers First Suggested Dismissing Prosecutors 2 Years Ago, Documents Show," *Washington Post*, March 13, 2007, p. Page A01. http://www.washingtonpost.com/wp-dyn/content/article/2007/03/12/AR2007031201818_pf.html

Laura Jakes Jordan, "Agency Weighed Prosecutors' Politics," ABC News, April 13, 2007. http://abcnews.go.com/Politics/wireStory?id=3039829

Kevin Johnson, "Prosecutor Fired So Ex-Rove Aide Could Get His Job," *USA Today*, February 6, 2007. http://www.usatoday.com/news/washington/2007-02-06-prosecutor-rove-aide_x.htm

Article XXVIII

David Johnston, "White House Is Reported to Be Linked to a Dismissal," *New York Times,* February 16, 2007. http://www.nytimes.com/2007/02/16/washington/16attorneys.html

CNN, "Subpoenas Target Justice; White House Could be Next," March 15, 2007. http://www.cnn.com/2007/POLITICS/03/15/fired.attorneys/index.html"

Sheryl Gay Stolberg, "Bush Clashes With Congress on Prosecutors," *New York Times*, March 20, 2007. http://www.nytimes.com/2007/03/21/us/politics/21attorneys.html?ex=1332129600&en=6190f05e97511f82&ei=5088&partner=rssnyt&emc=rss

President Bush Addresses Resignations of US Attorneys — The Diplomatic Reception Room. http://www.whitehouse.gov/news/releases/2007/03/20070320-8.html

Michael Roston, "Bush blocks Miers from appearing before House Judiciary Committee, Contempt Charges Possible," RawStory.com, July 11, 2007. http://rawstory.com/news/2007/BREAKING__Bush_blocks_Miers_from_0711.html

The *New York Times* Editorial, "Questions About a Governor's Fall," June 30, 2007. http://www.nytimes.com/2007/06/30/opinion/30sat2.html?ex=1340856000&en=6522ac53b9fc2a90&ei=5090&partner=rssuserland&emc=rss

Adam Cohen, "A Woman Wrongly Convicted and a US Attorney Who Kept His Job," *New York Times*, April, 16, 2007. http://www.nytimes.com/2007/04/16/opinion/16mon4.html

Article XXIX

CONSPIRACY TO VIOLATE THE VOTING RIGHTS ACT OF 1965

In his conduct while President of the United States, George W. Bush, in violation of his constitutional oath to faithfully execute the office of President of the United States and, to the best of his ability, preserve, protect, and defend the Constitution of the United States, and in violation of his constitutional duty under Article II, Section 3 of the Constitution "to take care that the laws be faithfully executed," has both personally and acting through his agents and subordinates, willfully corrupted and manipulated the electoral process of the United States for his personal gain and the personal gain of his co-conspirators and allies; violated the United States Constitution and law by failing to protect the civil rights of African-American voters and others in the 2004 Election, and impeded the right of the people to vote and have their vote properly and accurately counted, in that:

A. On November 5, 2002, and prior thereto, James Tobin, while serving as the regional director of the National Republican Senatorial Campaign Committee and as the New England Chairman of Bush-Cheney '04 Inc., did, at the direction of the White House under the administration of George W. Bush, along with other agents both known and unknown, commit unlawful acts by aiding and abetting a scheme to use computerized hang-up calls to jam phone lines set up by the New Hampshire Democratic Party and the Manchester firefighters' union on Election Day;

B. An investigation by the Democratic staff of the House Judiciary Committee into the voting procedures in Ohio during the 2004 election found "widespread instances of intimidation and misinformation in violation of the Voting Rights Act, the Civil Rights Act of 1968, Equal Protection, Due Process and the Ohio right to vote";

C. The 14th Amendment Equal Protection Clause guarantees that no minority group will suffer disparate treatment in a federal, state, or local election in stating that: "No State shall make or enforce any law which shall abridge the privileges or immunities of citizens of the United States; nor shall any State deprive any person of life, liberty, or property, without due process of law; nor deny to any person within its jurisdiction the equal protection of the laws." However, during and at various times of the year 2004, John Kenneth Blackwell, then serving as the Secretary of State for the State of Ohio and also serving simultaneously as Co-Chairman of the Committee to Re-Elect George W. Bush in the State of Ohio, did, at the direction of the White House under the administration of George W. Bush, along with other agents both known and unknown, commit unlawful acts in violation of the Equal Protection Clause of the 14th Amendment to the United States Constitution by failing to protect the voting rights of African-American citizens in Ohio and further, John Kenneth Blackwell did disenfranchise African-American voters under color of law, by

D. Willfully denying certain neighborhoods in the cities of Cleveland, Ohio and Columbus, Ohio, along with other urban areas in the State of Ohio, an adequate number of electronic voting machines and provisional paper ballots, thereby unlawfully impeding duly registered voters from the act of voting and thus violating the civil rights of an unknown number of United States citizens.

E. In Franklin County, George W. Bush and his agent, Ohio Secretary of State John Kenneth Blackwell, Co-Chair of the Bush-Cheney Re-election Campaign, failed to protect the rights of African-American voters by not properly investigating the withholding of 125 electronic voting machines assigned to the city of Columbus.

F. Forty-two African-American precincts in Columbus were each missing one voting machine that had been present in the 2004 primary.

G. African-American voters in the city of Columbus were forced to wait three to seven hours to vote in the 2004 presidential election.

H. Willfully issuing unclear and conflicting rules regarding the methods and manner of becoming a legally registered voter in the State of Ohio, and willfully issuing unclear and unnecessary edicts regarding the weight of paper registration forms legally acceptable to the State of Ohio, thereby creating confusion for both voters and voting officials and thus impeding the right of an unknown number of United States citizens to register and vote.

I. Ohio Secretary of State John Kenneth Blackwell directed through Advisory 2004-31 that voter registration forms, which were greatest in urban minority areas, should not be accepted and should be returned unless submitted on 80 bond paper weight. Blackwell's own office was found to be using 60 bond paper weight.

J. Willfully permitted and encouraged election officials in Cleveland, Cincinnati and Toledo to conduct a massive partisan purge of registered voter rolls, eventually expunging more than 300,000 voters, many of whom were duly registered voters, and who were thus deprived of their constitutional right to vote;

K. Between the 2000 and 2004 Ohio presidential elections, 24.93% of the voters in the city of Cleveland, a city with a majority of African American citizens, were purged from the voting rolls.

L. In that same period, the Ohio county of Miami, with census data indicating a 98% Caucasian population, refused to purge any voters from its rolls. Miami County "merged" voters from other surrounding counties into its voting rolls and even allowed voters from other states to vote.

M. In Toledo, Ohio, an urban city with a high African-American concentration, 28,000 voters were purged from the voting rolls in August of 2004, just prior to the presidential election. This purge was conducted under the control and direction of George W. Bush's agent, Ohio Secretary of State John Kenneth Blackwell outside of the regularly established cycle of purging voters in odd-numbered years.

N. Willfully allowing Ohio Secretary of State John Kenneth Blackwell, acting under color of law and as an agent of George W. Bush, to issue a directive that no votes would be counted unless cast in the right precinct, reversing Ohio's long-standing practice of counting votes for president if cast in the right county.

O. Willfully allowing his agent, Ohio Secretary of State John Kenneth Blackwell, the Co-Chair of the Bush-Cheney Re-election Campaign, to do nothing to assure the voting rights of 10,000 people in the city of Cleveland when a computer error by the private vendor Diebold Election Systems, Inc. incorrectly disenfranchised 10,000 voters

P. Willfully allowing his agent, Ohio Secretary of State John Kenneth Blackwell, the Co-Chair of the Bush-Cheney Re-election Campaign, to ensure that uncounted and provisional ballots in Ohio's 2004 presidential election would be disproportionately concentrated in urban African-American districts.

Q. In Ohio's Lucas County, which includes Toledo, 3,122 or 41.13% of the provisional ballots went uncounted under the direction of George W. Bush's agent, the Secretary of State of Ohio, John Kenneth Blackwell, Co-Chair of the Committee to Re-Elect Bush/Cheney in Ohio.

R. In Ohio's Cuyahoga County, which includes Cleveland, 8,559 or 32.82% of the provisional ballots went uncounted.

S. In Ohio's Hamilton County, which includes Cincinnati, 3,529 or 24.23% of the provisional ballots went uncounted.

T. Statewide, the provisional ballot rejection rate was 9% as compared to the greater figures in the urban areas.

U. The Department of Justice, charged with enforcing the Voting Rights Act of 1965, the 14th Amendment's Equal Protection Clause, and other voting rights laws in the United States of America, under the direction and Administration of George W. Bush did willfully and purposely obstruct and stonewall legitimate criminal investigations into myriad cases of reported electoral fraud and suppression in the state of Ohio. Such activities, carried out by the department on behalf of George W. Bush in counties such as Franklin and Knox by persons such as John K. Tanner and others, were meant to confound and whitewash legitimate legal criminal investigations into the suppression of massive numbers of legally registered voters and the removal of their right to cast a ballot fairly and freely in the state of Ohio, which was crucial to the certified electoral victory of George W. Bush in 2004.

V. On or about November 1, 2006, members of the United States Department of Justice, under the control and direction of the Administration of George W. Bush, brought indictments for voter registration fraud within days of an election, in order to directly effect the outcome of that election for partisan purposes, and in doing so, thereby violated the Justice Department's own rules against filing election-related indictments close to an election;

X. Emails have been obtained showing that the Republican National Committee and members of Bush-Cheney '04 Inc., did, at the direction of the White House under the administration of George W. Bush, engage in voter suppression in five states by a method know as "vote caging," an illegal voter suppression technique;

Y. Agents of George W. Bush, including Mark F. "Thor" Hearne, the national general counsel of Bush/Cheney '04, Inc., did, at the behest of George W. Bush, as members of a criminal front group, distribute known false information and propaganda in the hopes of forwarding legislation and other actions that would result in the disenfranchisement of Democratic voters for partisan purposes. The scheme, run under the auspices of an organization known as "The American Center for Voting Rights" (ACVR), was funded by agents of George W. Bush in violation of laws governing tax exempt 501(c)3 organizations and in violation of federal laws forbidding the distribution of such propaganda by the federal government and agents working on its behalf.

Z. Members of the United States Department of Justice, under the control and direction of the Administration of George W. Bush, did, for partisan reasons, illegally and with malice aforethought block career attorneys and other officials in the Department of Justice from filing three lawsuits charging local and county governments with violating the voting rights of African-Americans and other minorities, according to seven former senior United States Justice Department employees.

AA. Members of the United States Department of Justice, under the control and direction of the Administration of George W. Bush, did illegally and with malice aforethought derail at least two investigations into possible voter discrimination, according to a letter sent to the Senate Rules and Administration Committee and written by former employees of the United States Department of Justice, Voting Rights Section.

BB. Members of the United States Election Assistance Commission (EAC), under the control and direction of the Administration of George W. Bush, have purposefully and willfully misled the public, in violation of several laws, by;

CC. Withholding from the public and then altering a legally mandated report on the true measure and threat of Voter Fraud, as commissioned by the EAC and completed in June 2006, prior to the 2006 mid-term election, but withheld from release prior to that election when its information would have been useful in the administration of elections across the country, because the results of the statutorily required and tax-payer funded report did not conform with the illegal, partisan propaganda efforts and politicized agenda of the Bush Administration;

DD. Withholding from the public a legally mandated report on the disenfranchising effect of Photo Identification laws at the polling place, shown to disproportionately disenfranchise voters not of George W. Bush's political party. The report was commissioned by the EAC and completed in June 2006, prior to the 2006 mid-term election, but withheld from release prior to that election when its information would have been useful in the administration of elections across the country.

EE. Withholding from the public a legally mandated report on the effectiveness of Provisional Voting as commissioned by the EAC and completed in June 2006, prior to the 2006 mid-term election, but withheld from release prior to that election when its information would have been useful in the administration of elections across the country, and keeping that report unreleased for more than a year until it was revealed by independent media outlets.

For directly harming the rights and manner of suffrage, for suffering to make them secret and unknowable, for overseeing and participating in the disenfranchisement of legal voters, for instituting debates and doubts about the true nature of elections, all against the will and consent of local voters affected, and forced through threats of litigation by agents and agencies overseen by George W. Bush, the actions of Mr. Bush to do the opposite of securing and guaranteeing the right of the people to alter or abolish their government via the electoral process, being a violation of an inalienable right, and an immediate threat to Liberty.

In all of these actions and decisions, President George W. Bush has acted in a manner contrary to his trust as President, and subversive of constitutional government, to the prejudice of the cause of law and justice and to the manifest injury of the people of the United States. Wherefore, President George W. Bush, by such conduct, is guilty of an impeachable offense warranting removal from office.

Article XXIX notes

James Tobin and his election plots for George W. Bush. http://www.sourcewatch.org/index.php?title=James_Tobin

House Judiciary Committee Report, January 5, 2005. http://www.truthout.org/docs_05/010605Y.shtml

Robert F. Kennedy Jr., "Was the 2004 Election Stolen?," Rolling Stone, June, 2006. http://www.rolling-stone.com/news/story/10432334/was_the_2004_election_stolen/print .

Jim Bebbington and Laura Bischoff, "Ohio Secretary of State Blocks New Voter Registrations," Dayton Daily News, September 28, 2004. http://www.truthout.org/docs_04/092904W.shtml

Brad Friedman, "DOJ WHITEWASHES OHIO ELECTION INVESTIGATION! CONYERS 'FLABBERGASTED' IN REBUTTAL!," BradBlog.com. http://www.bradblog.com/?p=1513

Paul Kiel, "Controversial USA Delivered 'Voter Fraud' Indictments Right on Time," TPM Muckraker, May 1, 2007. http://www.tpmmuckraker.com/archives/003107.php

Jason Leopold and Matt Renner, "Emails Detail RNC Voter Suppression in Five States," truthout.org. http://www.truthout.org/docs_2006/072607A.shtml

The 35 Articles of Impeachment

Thor Hearne, "American Center for Voting Rights" (ACVR) GOP 'Voter Fraud' Scam. http://www.bradblog.com/?page_id=4418

Greg Gordon, "Justice Official Accused of Blocking Suits into Alleged Violations, McClatchy Newspapers, June 18, 2007. http://www.mcclatchydc.com/200/story/17102.html

Arlen Parsa, "US Election Assistance Commission Altered Final Report On 'Voter Fraud' For Political Purposes, BradBlog.com, April 11, 2007. http://www.bradblog.com/?p=4391

Brad Friedman, "EAC Finally Releases Previously Withheld, 9 Month Old Report on 'Voter ID' Concerns After Congressional Prodding, BradBlog.com. http://www.bradblog.com/?p=4341

Rick Hasen, "Another Report to the EAC Buried?, Election Law Blog, December 2, 2007. http://election-lawblog.org/archives/009837.html

Voting Rights Act of 1965. ourdocuments.gov http://www.ourdocuments.gov/doc.php?doc=100&page=transcript

Article XXX

MISLEADING CONGRESS AND THE AMERICAN PEOPLE IN AN ATTEMPT TO DESTROY MEDICARE

In his conduct while President of the United States, George W. Bush, in violation of his constitutional oath to faithfully execute the office of President of the United States and, to the best of his ability, preserve, protect, and defend the Constitution of the United States, and in violation of his constitutional duty under Article II, Section 3 of the Constitution "to take care that the laws be faithfully executed," has both personally and acting through his agents and subordinates, together with the Vice President, pursued policies which deliberately drained the fiscal resources of Medicare by forcing it to compete with subsidized private insurance plans which are allowed to arbitrarily select or not select those they will cover; failing to provide reasonable levels of reimbursements to Medicare providers, thereby discouraging providers from participating in the program, and designing a Medicare Part D benefit without cost controls which allowed pharmaceutical companies to gouge the American taxpayers for the price of prescription drugs.

The President created, manipulated, and disseminated information given to the citizens and Congress of the United States in support of his prescription drug plan for Medicare that enriched drug companies while failing to save beneficiaries sufficient money on their prescription drugs. He misled Congress and the American people into thinking the cost of the benefit was $400 billion. It was widely understood that if the cost exceeded that amount, the bill would not pass due to concerns about fiscal irresponsibility.

A Medicare Actuary who possessed information regarding the true cost of the plan, $539 billion, was instructed by the Medicare Administrator to deny Congressional requests for it. The Actuary was threatened with sanctions if the information was disclosed to Congress, which, unaware of the information, approved the bill. Despite the fact that official cost estimates far exceeded $400 billion, President Bush offered assurances to Congress that the cost was $400 billion, when his office had information to the contrary. In the House of Representatives, the bill passed by a single vote and the Conference Report passed by only five votes. The White House knew the actual cost of the drug benefit was high enough to prevent its passage. Yet the White House concealed the truth and impeded an investigation into its culpability.

In all of these actions and decisions, President George W. Bush has acted in a manner contrary to his trust as President, and subversive of constitutional government, to the prejudice of the cause of law and justice and to the manifest injury of the people of the United States. Wherefore, President George W. Bush, by such conduct, is guilty of an impeachable offense warranting removal from office.

Article XXX notes

Trudy Lieberman, "Part D From Outer Space, *The Nation*, January 30, 2006. http://www.thenation.com/doc/20060130/lieberman

Trudy Lieberman, "Privatizing Medicare," *The Nation*, July 7, 2003. http://www.thenation.com/doc/20060130/lieberman

intensity has increased with oceanic surface temperatures over the past 30 years. The physics of hurricane intensity growth ... has clarified and explained the thermodynamic basis for these observations. [Kerry] Emanuel has tested this relationship and presented convincing evidence."

FEMA's 2001 list of the top three most likely and most devastating disasters were a San Francisco earthquake, a terrorist attack on New York, and a Category 4 hurricane hitting New Orleans, with New Orleans being the number one item on that list. FEMA conducted a five-day hurricane simulation exercise in 2004, "Hurricane Pam," mimicking a Katrina-like event. This exercise combined the National Weather Service, the US Army Corps of Engineers, the LSU Hurricane Center and other state and federal agencies, resulting in the development of emergency response plans. The exercise demonstrated, among other things, that thousands of mainly indigent New Orleans residents would be unable to evacuate on their own. They would need substantial government assistance. These plans, however, were not implemented in part due to the President's slashing of funds for protection. In the year before Hurricane Katrina hit, the President continued to cut budgets and deny grants to the Gulf Coast. In June of 2004 the Army Corps of Engineers levee budget for New Orleans was cut, and it was cut again in June of 2005, this time by $71.2 million or a whopping 44% of the budget. As a result, ACE was forced to suspend any repair work on the levees. In 2004 FEMA denied a Louisiana disaster mitigation grant request.

The President was given multiple warnings that Hurricane Katrina had a high likelihood of causing serious damage to New Orleans and the Gulf Coast. At 10 AM on Sunday 28 August 2005, the day before the storm hit, the National Weather Service published an alert titled "DEVASTATING DAMAGE EXPECTED." Printed in all capital letters, the alert stated that "MOST OF THE AREA WILL BE UNINHABITABLE FOR WEEKS...PERHAPS LONGER. AT LEAST ONE HALF OF WELL CONSTRUCTED HOMES WILL HAVE ROOF AND WALL FAILURE. ... POWER OUTAGES WILL LAST FOR WEEKS. ... WATER SHORTAGES WILL MAKE HUMAN SUFFERING INCREDIBLE BY MODERN STANDARDS."

The Homeland Security Department also briefed the President on the scenario, warning of levee breaches and severe flooding. According to the *New York Times*," a Homeland Security Department report submitted to the White House at 1:47 a.m. on Aug. 29, hours before the storm hit, said, 'Any storm rated Category 4 or greater will likely lead to severe flooding and/or levee breaching.'" These warnings clearly contradict the statements made by President Bush immediately after the storm that such devastation could not have been predicted. On 1 September 2005 the President said "I don't think anyone anticipated the breach of the levees."

The President's response to Katrina via FEMA and DHS was criminally delayed, indifferent, and inept. The only FEMA employee posted in New Orleans in the immediate aftermath of Hurricane Katrina, Marty Bahamonde, emailed head of FEMA Michael Brown from his Blackberry device on August 31, 2005 regarding the conditions. The email was urgent and detailed and indicated that "The situation is past critical…Estimates are many will die within hours." Brown's reply was emblematic of the administration's entire response to the catastrophe: "Thanks for the update. Anything specific I need to do or tweak?" The Secretary of Homeland Security, Michael Chertoff, did not declare an emergency, did not mobilize the federal resources, and seemed to not even know what was happening on the ground until reporters told him.

On Friday August 26, 2005, Governor Kathleen Blanco declared a State of Emergency in Louisiana and Governor Haley Barbour of Mississippi followed suit the next day. Also on that Saturday, Governor Blanco asked the President to declare a Federal State of Emergency, and on 28 August 2005, the Sunday before the storm hit, Mayor Nagin declared a State of Emergency in New Orleans. This shows that the local authorities, responding to federal warnings, knew how bad the destruction was going to be and anticipated being overwhelmed. Failure to act under these circumstances demonstrates gross negligence.

In all of these actions and decisions, President George W. Bush has acted in a manner contrary to his trust as President, and subversive of constitutional government, to the prejudice of the cause of law and justice and to the manifest injury of the people of the United States. Wherefore, President George W. Bush, by such conduct, is guilty of an impeachable offense warranting removal from office.

Article XXXI notes

FEMA Predicted a "Catastrophic Hurricane" Could Strike New Orleans and Cause a "Mega-Disaster," House Committee on Oversight and Government Reform. http://oversight.house.gov/story.asp?ID=922

"Democrats: Katrina E-mails Show Levee Breaches Reported Early," CNN, February 13, 2006. http://www.cnn.com/2006/POLITICS/02/10/katrina.levees/index.html

The 35 Articles of Impeachment

"Duke Students Beat Feds in Aiding Stranded Victims," CNN, September 7, 2005. http://transcripts.cnn.com/TRANSCRIPTS/0509/06/asb.01.html

Michael Laris and Karin Brulliard, "Bad Communication Hinders Area's Aid Efforts," *Washington Post*, September 3, 2005. http://www.washingtonpost.com/wp-dyn/content/article/2005/09/02/AR2005090202363.html

Eric Lipton, Christopher Drew, Scott Shane and David Rohde, "Breakdowns Marked Path From Hurricane to Anarchy," *New York Times*, September 11, 2005. http://www.nytimes.com/2005/09/11/national/nationalspecial/11response.html

Robin Wallace, "At Shelters, Katrina Health Crisis Continues," Fox News, September 6, 2005. http://www.foxnews.com/story/0,2933,168519,00.html

Daren Fonda and Rita Healy, "How Reliable Is Brown's Resume?" *Time*, September 8, 2005. http://www.time.com/time/nation/article/0,8599,1103003,00.html

Adam Nagourney and Carl Hulse, "Democrats Step Up Criticism of White House," *New York Times*, September 8, 2005. http://www.nytimes.com/2005/09/08/national/nationalspecial/08democrats.html

Article XXXII

MISLEADING CONGRESS AND THE AMERICAN PEOPLE, SYTEMATICALLY UNDERMINING EFFORTS TO ADDRESS GLOBAL CLIMATE CHANGE.

In his conduct while President of the United States, George W. Bush, in violation of his constitutional oath to faithfully execute the office of President of the United States and, to the best of his ability, preserve, protect, and defend the Constitution of the United States, and in violation of his constitutional duty under Article II, Section 3 of the Constitution "to take care that the laws be faithfully executed," has both personally and acting through his agents and subordinates, together with the Vice President, ignored the peril to life and property posed by global climate change, manipulated scientific information and mishandled protective policy, constituting nonfeasance and malfeasance in office, abuse of power, dereliction of duty, and deception of Congress and the American people.

President Bush knew the expected effects of climate change and the role of human activities in driving climate change. This knowledge preceded his first Presidential term.

1. During his 2000 Presidential campaign, he promised to regulate carbon dioxide emissions.

2. In 2001, the Intergovernmental Panel on Climate Change, a global body of hundreds of the world's foremost experts on climate change, concluded that "most of observed warming over last 50 years (is) likely due to increases in greenhouse gas concentrations due to human activities." The Third Assessment Report projected several effects of climate change such as continued "widespread retreat" of glaciers, an "increase threats to human health, particularly in lower income populations, predominantly within tropical/subtropical countries," and "water shortages."

3. The grave danger to national security posed by global climate change was recognized by the Pentagon's Defense Advanced Planning Research

Projects Agency in October of 2003. An agency-commissioned report "explores how such an abrupt climate change scenario could potentially de-stabilize the geo-political environment, leading to skirmishes, battles, and even war due to resource constraints such as: 1) Food shortages due to decreases in net global agricultural production 2) Decreased availability and quality of fresh water in key regions due to shifted precipitation patters, causing more frequent floods and droughts 3) Disrupted access to energy supplies due to extensive sea ice and storminess."

4. A December 2004 paper in *Science* reviewed 928 studies published in peer reviewed journals to determine the number providing evidence against the existence of a link between anthropogenic emissions of carbon dioxide and climate change. "Remarkably, none of the papers disagreed with the consensus position."

5. The November 2007 Inter-Governmental Panel on Climate Change (IPCC) Fourth Assessment Report showed that global anthropogenic emissions of greenhouse gasses have increased 70% between 1970 and 2004, and anthropogenic emissions are very likely the cause of global climate change. The report concluded that global climate change could cause the extinction of 20 to 30 percent of species in unique ecosystems such as the polar areas and biodiversity hotspots, increase extreme weather events especially in the developing world, and have adverse effects on food production and fresh water availability.

The President has done little to address this most serious of problems, thus constituting an abuse of power and criminal neglect. He has also actively endeavored to undermine efforts by the federal government, states, and other nations to take action on their own.

1. In March 2001, President Bush announced the US would not be pursuing ratification of the Kyoto Protocol, an international effort to reduce greenhouse gasses. The United States is the only industrialized nation that has failed to ratify the accord.

2. In March0f 2008, Representative Henry Waxman wrote to EPA Administrator Stephen Johnson: "In August 2003, the Bush Administration denied a petition to regulate CO^2 emissions from motor vehicles by deciding that CO^2 was not a pollutant under the Clean Air Act. In April 2007, the US Supreme Court overruled that determination in Massachusetts v. EPA. The Supreme Court wrote that 'If EPA makes a finding of endangerment, the Clean Air Act requires the agency to regulate emissions of the deleterious

pollutant from new motor vehicles.' The EPA then conducted an extensive investigation involving 60-70 staff who concluded that 'CO_2 emissions endanger both human health and welfare.' These findings were submitted to the White House, after which work on the findings and the required regulations was halted."

3. A Memo to Members of the Committee on Oversight and Government Reform on May 19, 2008 stated "The record before the Committee shows: (1) the career staff at EPA unanimously supported granting California's petition (to be allowed to regulate greenhouse gas emissions from cars and trucks, consistent with California state law); (2) Stephen Johnson, the Administrator of EPA, also supported granting California's petition at least in part; and (3) Administrator Johnson reversed his position after communications with officials in the White House."

The President has suppressed the release of scientific information related to global climate change, an action which undermines Congress' ability to legislate and provide oversight, and which has thwarted efforts to prevent global climate change despite the serious threat that it poses.

1. In February, 2001, ExxonMobil wrote a memo to the White House outlining ways to influence the outcome of the Third Assessment report by the Intergovernmental Panel on Climate Change. The memo opposed the reelection of Dr. Robert Watson as the IPCC Chair. The White House then supported an opposition candidate, who was subsequently elected to replace Dr. Watson.

2. *The New York Times* on January 29, 2006, reported that James Hansen, NASA's senior climate scientist was warned of "dire consequences" if he continued to speak out about global climate change and the need for reducing emissions of associated gasses. The *Times* also reported that: "At climate laboratories of the National Oceanic and Atmospheric Administration, for example, many scientists who routinely took calls from reporters five years ago can now do so only if the interview is approved by administration officials in Washington, and then only if a public affairs officer is present or on the phone."

3. In December of 2007, the House Committee on Oversight and Government Reform issued a report based on 16 months of investigation and 27,000 pages of documentation. According to the summary: "The evidence before the Committee leads to one inescapable conclusion: the Bush Administration has engaged in a systematic effort to manipulate

climate change science and mislead policy makers and the public about the dangers of global warming." The report described how the White House appointed former petroleum industry lobbyist Phil Cooney as head of the Council on Environmental Quality. The report states "There was a systematic White House effort to minimize the significance of climate change by editing climate change reports. CEQ Chief of Staff Phil Cooney and other CEQ officials made at least 294 edits to the Administration's Strategic Plan of the Climate Change Science Program to exaggerate or emphasize scientific uncertainties or to de-emphasize or diminish the importance of the human role in global warming."

4. On April 23, 2008, Representative Henry Waxman wrote a letter to EPA Administrator Stephen L Johnson. In it he reported: "Almost 1,600 EPA scientists completed the Union of Concerned Scientists survey questionnaire. Over 22 percent of these scientists reported that 'selective or incomplete use of data to justify a specific regulatory outcome' occurred 'frequently' or 'occasionally' at EPA. Ninety-four EPA scientists reported being frequently or occasionally directed to inappropriately exclude or alter technical information from an EPA scientific document. Nearly 200 EPA scientists said that they have frequently or occasionally been in situations in which scientists have actively objected to, resigned from or removed themselves from a project because of pressure to change scientific findings."

In all of these actions and decisions, President George W. Bush has acted in a manner contrary to his trust as President and subversive of constitutional government, to the prejudice of the cause of law and justice and to the manifest injury of the people of the United States. Wherefore, President George W. Bush, by such conduct, is guilty of an impeachable offense warranting removal from office.

Article XXXII notes

Peter Schwartz and Doug Randall, "An Abrupt Climate Change Scenario and Its Implications for US National Security," October, 2003. http://www.gbn.com/GBNDocumentDisplayServlet. srv?aid=26231&url=/UploadDocumentDisplayServlet.srv?id=28566

Bush Defends Rejection of Kyoto Treaty, UPI, March 30, 2001. http://archive.newsmax.com/archives/articles/2001/3/29/164418.shtml

Text of a Letter from the President to Senators Hagel, Helms, Craig, and Roberts, March 13, 2001. http://www.whitehouse.gov/news/releases/2001/03/20010314.html

IPCC Fourth Assessment Report: Climate Change 2007. http://www.ipcc.ch/ipccreports/assessments-reports.htm

IPCC Third Assessment Report: Climate Change 2001. http://www.ipcc.ch/ipccreports/assessments-reports.htm

IPCC Second Assessment Report: Climate Change 1995. http://www.ipcc.ch/ipccreports/assessments-reports.htm

Andrew C. Revkin, "Climate Expert Says NASA Tried to Silence Him," *New York Times*, January 29, 2006. http://www.nytimes.com/2006/01/29/science/earth/29climate.html

Article XXXIII

REPEATEDLY IGNORED AND FAILED TO RESPOND
TO HIGH LEVEL INTELLIGENCE WARNINGS OF PLANNED
TERRORIST ATTACKS IN THE US, PRIOR TO 9/11

In his conduct while President of the United States, George W. Bush, in violation of his constitutional oath to faithfully execute the office of President of the United States and, to the best of his ability, preserve, protect, and defend the Constitution of the United States, and in violation of his constitutional duty under Article II, Section 3 of the Constitution "to take care that the laws be faithfully executed," has both personally and acting through his agents and subordinates, together with the Vice President, failed in his Constitutional duties to take proper steps to protect the nation prior to September 11, 2001.

The White House's top counter-terrorism adviser, Richard A. Clarke, has testified that from the beginning of George W. Bush's presidency until September 11, 2001, Clarke attempted unsuccessfully to persuade President Bush to take steps to protect the nation against terrorism. Clarke sent a memorandum to then-National Security Advisor Condoleezza Rice on January 24, 2001, "urgently" but unsuccessfully requesting "a Cabinet-level meeting to deal with the impending al Qaeda attack."

In April 2001, Clarke was finally granted a meeting, but only with second-in-command department representatives, including Deputy Secretary of Defense Paul Wolfowitz, who made light of Clarke's concerns.

Clarke confirms that in June, July, and August, 2001, the Central Intelligence Agency (CIA) warned the president in daily briefings of unprecedented indications that a major al Qaeda attack was going to happen against the United States somewhere in the world in the weeks and months ahead. Yet, Clarke was still unable to convene a cabinet-level meeting to address the issue.

Condoleezza Rice has testified that George Tenet met with the president

40 times to warn him that a major al-Qaeda attack was going to take place, and that in response the president did not convene any meetings of top officials. At such meetings, the FBI could have shared information on possible terrorists enrolled at flight schools. Among the many preventive steps that could have been taken, the Federal Aviation Administration, airlines, and airports might have been put on full alert.

According to Condoleezza Rice, the first and only cabinet-level meeting prior to 9/11 to discuss the threat of terrorist attacks took place on September 4, 2001, one week before the attacks in New York and Washington.

On August 6, 2001, President Bush was presented a President's Daily Brief (PDB) article titled "Bin Laden Determined to Strike in US" The lead sentence of that PDB article indicated that Bin Laden and his followers wanted to "follow the example of World Trade Center bomber Ramzi Yousef and 'bring the fighting to America.'" The article warned: "Al-Qa'ida members—including some who are US citizens—have resided in or traveled to the US for years, and the group apparently maintains a support structure that could aid attacks."

The article cited a "more sensational threat reporting that Bin Laden wanted to hijack a US aircraft," but indicated that the CIA had not been able to corroborate such reporting. The PDB item included information from the FBI indicating "patterns of suspicious activity in this country consistent with preparations for hijackings or other types of attacks, including recent surveillance of federal buildings in New York." The article also noted that the CIA and FBI were investigating "a call to our embassy in the UAE in May saying that a group of Bin Laden supporters was in the US planning attacks with explosives."

The president spent the rest of August 6, and almost all the rest of August 2001 on vacation. There is no evidence that he called any meetings of his advisers to discuss this alarming report. When the title and substance of this PDB article were later reported in the press, then-National Security Adviser Condoleezza Rice began a sustained campaign to play down its significance, until the actual text was eventually released by the White House.

New York Times writer Douglas Jehl, put it this way: "In a single 17-sentence document, the intelligence briefing delivered to President Bush in August 2001 spells out the who, hints at the what and points towards the where of the terrorist attacks on New York and Washington that followed 36 days later."

Eleanor Hill, Executive Director of the joint congressional committee investigating the performance of the US intelligence community before September 11, 2001, reported in mid-September 2002 that intelligence reports a year earlier "reiterated a consistent and constant theme: Osama bin Laden's intent to launch terrorist attacks inside the United States."

That joint inquiry revealed that just two months before September 11, an intelligence briefing for "senior government officials" predicted a terrorist attack with these words: "The attack will be spectacular and designed to inflict mass casualties against US facilities or interests. Attack preparations have been made. Attack will occur with little or no warning."

Given the White House's insistence on secrecy with regard to what intelligence was given to President Bush, the joint-inquiry report does not divulge whether he took part in that briefing. Even if he did not, it strains credulity to suppose that those "senior government officials" would have kept its alarming substance from the president.

Again, there is no evidence that the president held any meetings or took any action to deal with the threats of such attacks.

In all of these actions and decisions, President George W. Bush has acted in a manner contrary to his trust as President, and subversive of constitutional government, to the prejudice of the cause of law and justice and to the manifest injury of the people of the United States. Wherefore, President George W. Bush, by such conduct, is guilty of an impeachable offense warranting removal from office.

Article XXXIII notes

Douglas Jehl, "A Warning, but Clear? White House Tries to Make the Point That New Details Add Up to Old News," *New York Times*, April 11, 2004, p. A13.

"What did Bush Know Pre-Sept. 11?," *Miami Herald*, September 25, 2002.

CIA, President's Daily Brief article "Bin Laden Determined to Strike in US," declassified and approved for release by White House, April 10, 2004.

Condoleezza Rice, "Sworn Testimony to 9/11 Commission," *New York Times*, April 8, 2004. http://www.nytimes.com/2004/04/08/politics/08RICE-TEXT.html?ex=1211083200&en=73c66064d671499f&ei=5070

Article XXXIV

OBSTRUCTION OF INVESTIGATION
INTO THE ATTACKS OF SEPTEMBER 11, 2001

In his conduct while President of the United States, George W. Bush, in violation of his constitutional oath to faithfully execute the office of President of the United States and, to the best of his ability, preserve, protect, and defend the Constitution of the United States, and in violation of his constitutional duty under Article II, Section 3 of the Constitution "to take care that the laws be faithfully executed," has both personally and acting through his agents and subordinates, together with the Vice President, obstructed investigations into the attacks on the World Trade Center and Pentagon on September 11, 2001.

Following September 11, 2001, President Bush and Vice President Cheney took strong steps to thwart any and all proposals that the circumstances of the attack be addressed. Then-Secretary of State Colin Powell was forced to renege on his public promise on September 23 that a "White Paper" would be issued to explain the circumstances. Less than two weeks after that promise, Powell apologized for his "unfortunate choice of words," and explained that Americans would have to rely on "information coming out in the press and in other ways."

On Sept. 26, 2001, President Bush drove to Central Intelligence Agency (CIA) headquarters in Langley, Virginia, stood with Director of Central Intelligence George Tenet and said: "My report to the nation is, we've got the best intelligence we can possibly have thanks to the men and women of the CIA." George Tenet subsequently and falsely claimed not to have visited the president personally between the start of Bush's long Crawford vacation and September 11, 2001.

Testifying before the 9/11 Commission on April 14, 2004, Tenet answered a question from Commission member Timothy Roemer by referring to the president's vacation (July 29-August 30) in Crawford and insisting that he did not see the president at all in August 2001. "You never talked with him?" Roemer asked. "No," Tenet replied, explaining that for much of August he too was "on leave." An Agency spokesman called reporters that same evening to say Tenet had misspoken, and that Tenet had briefed Bush on August 17 and 31. The spokesman explained that the second briefing took place after the president had returned to Washington, and played down the first one, in Crawford, as uneventful.

In his book, *At the Center of the Storm*, (2007) Tenet, refers to what is almost certainly his August 17 visit to Crawford as a follow-up to the "Bin Laden Determined to Strike in the US" article in the CIA-prepared President's Daily Brief of August 6. That briefing was immortalized in a *Time* magazine photo capturing Harriet Myers holding the PDB open for the president, as two CIA officers sit by. It is the same briefing to which the president reportedly reacted by telling the CIA briefer, "All right, you've covered your ass now." (Ron Suskind, The One-Percent Doctrine, p. 2, 2006). In *At the Center of the Storm*, Tenet writes: "A few weeks after the August 6 PDB was delivered, I followed it to Crawford to make sure that the president stayed current on events."

A White House press release suggests Tenet was also there a week later, on August 24. According to the August 25, 2001, release, President Bush, addressing a group of visitors to Crawford on August 25, told them: "George Tenet and I, yesterday, we piled in the new nominees for the Chairman of the Joint Chiefs, the Vice Chairman and their wives and went right up the canyon."

In early February, 2002, Vice President Dick Cheney warned then-Senate Majority Leader Tom Daschle that if Congress went ahead with an investigation, administration officials might not show up to testify. As pressure grew for an investigation, the president and vice president agreed to the establishment of a congressional joint committee to conduct a "Joint Inquiry." Eleanor Hill, Executive Director of the Inquiry, opened the Joint Inquiry's final public hearing in mid-September 2002 with the following disclaimer: "I need to report that, according to the White House and the Director of Central Intelligence, the president's knowledge of intelligence information relevant to this inquiry remains classified, even when the substance of the intelligence information has been declassified."

The National Commission on Terrorist Attacks, also known as the 9/11 Commission, was created on November 27, 2002, following the passage of congressional legislation signed into law by President Bush. The President was asked to testify before the Commission. He refused to testify except for one hour in private with only two Commission members, with no oath administered, with no recording or note taking, and with the Vice President at his side. Commission Co-Chair Lee Hamilton has written that he believes the commission was set up to fail, was underfunded, was rushed, and did not receive proper cooperation and access to information.

A December 2007 review of classified documents by former members of the Commission found that the commission had made repeated and detailed requests to the CIA in 2003 and 2004 for documents and other information about the interrogation of operatives of Al Qaeda, and had been told falsely by a top CIA official that the agency had "produced or made available for review" everything that had been requested.

In all of these actions and decisions, President George W. Bush has acted in a manner contrary to his trust as President, and subversive of constitutional government, to the prejudice of the cause of law and justice and to the manifest injury of the people of the United States. Wherefore, President George W. Bush, by such conduct, is guilty of an impeachable offense warranting removal from office.

Article XXXIV notes

Dan Eggen, "9/11 Panel Suspected Deception by Pentagon, Allegations Brought to Inspectors General," *Washington Post*, August 2, 2006. http://www.washingtonpost.com/wp-dyn/content/article/2006/08/01/AR2006080101300.html

White House Press Release, August 25, 2001. http://www.whitehouse.gov/news/releases/2001/08/20010825-2.html

President George W. Bush, Remarks to CIA Workforce, September 26, 2001. https://www.cia.gov/news-information/speeches-testimony/2001/bush_speech_09262001.html

George Tenet, Testimony Before the 9/11 Commission, April 14, 2004. http://topics.nytimes.com/2004/04/14/politics/14TEXT-PANEL.html?ei=5070&en=6c53bb17b1f8447b&ex=1211083200&adxnnl=1&adxnnlx=1210990381-IRIukKHIXiY1c6ac/ff03g

Condoleezza Rice, "Sworn Testimony to 9/11 Commission," April 8, 2004. http://www.nytimes.com/2004/04/08/politics/08RICE-TEXT.html?ex=1211083200&en=73c66064d671499f&ei=5070

CIA Terrorist Threat Review: DCI Update, 23 August 2001. http://www.vaed.uscourts.gov/notablecases/moussaoui/exhibits/defense/660.pdf

CIA Terrorist Threat Review: DCI Update, 30 August 2001. http://www.vaed.uscourts.gov/notablecases/moussaoui/exhibits/defense/672.pdf

Article XXXV

ENDANGERING THE HEALTH OF 9/11 FIRST RESPONDERS

In his conduct while President of the United States, George W. Bush, in violation of his constitutional oath to faithfully execute the office of President of the United States and, to the best of his ability, preserve, protect, and defend the Constitution of the United States, and in violation of his constitutional duty under Article II, Section 3 of the Constitution "to take care that the laws be faithfully executed," has both personally and acting through his agents and subordinates, together with the Vice President, recklessly endangered the health of first responders, residents, and workers at and near the former location of the World Trade Center in New York City.

The Inspector General of the Environmental Protection Agency (EPA) August 21, 2003, report numbered 2003-P-00012 and entitled "EPA's Response to the World Trade Center Collapse: Challenges, Successes, and Areas for Improvement," includes the following findings:

"[W]hen EPA made a September 18 announcement that the air was 'safe' to breathe, it did not have sufficient data and analyses to make such a blanket statement. At that time, air monitoring data was lacking for several pollutants of concern, including particulate matter and polychlorinated biphenyls (PCBs). Furthermore, The White House Council on Environmental Quality (CEQ) influenced, through the collaboration process, the information that EPA communicated to the public through its early press releases when it convinced EPA to add reassuring statements and delete cautionary ones."

"As a result of the White House CEQ's influence, guidance for cleaning indoor spaces and information about the potential health effects from WTC debris were not included in EPA-issued press releases. In addition, based on CEQ's influence, reassuring information was added to at least one press release and cautionary information was deleted from EPA's draft version of that press release.... The White House's role in EPA's public communications about WTC environmental conditions was described in a September 12,

2001, e-mail from the EPA Deputy Administrator's Chief of Staff to senior EPA officials:

"'All statements to the media should be cleared through the NSC [National Security Council] before they are released.'

"According to the EPA Chief of Staff, one particular CEQ official was designated to work with EPA to ensure that clearance was obtained through NSC. The Associate Administrator for the EPA Office of Communications, Education, and Media Relations (OCEMR) said that no press release could be issued for a 3- to 4-week period after September 11 without approval from the CEQ contact."

Acting EPA Administrator Marianne Horinko, who sat in on EPA meetings with the White House has said in an interview that the White House played a coordinating role. The National Security Council played the key role, filtering incoming data on ground zero air and water, Horinko said: "I think that the thinking was, these are experts in WMD (weapons of mass destruction), so they should have the coordinating role."

In the cleanup of the Pentagon following September 11, 2001, Occupational Safety and Health Administration laws were enforced, and no workers became ill. At the World Trade Center site, the same laws were not enforced.

In the years since the release of the EPA Inspector General's above-cited report, the Bush Administration has still not effected a clean-up of the indoor air in apartments and workspaces near the site.

Screenings conducted at the Mount Sinai Medical Center and released in the September 10, 2004, Morbidity and Mortality Weekly Report (MMWR) of the federal Centers For Disease Control and Prevention (CDC), produced the following results:

"Both upper and lower respiratory problems and mental health difficulties are widespread among rescue and recovery workers who dug through the ruins of the World Trade Center in the days following its destruction in the attack of September 11, 2001.

"An analysis of the screenings of 1,138 workers and volunteers who responded to the World Trade Center disaster found that nearly three-quarters of them experienced new or worsened upper respiratory problems at some point while working at Ground Zero. And half of those examined had upper and/or lower respiratory symptoms that persisted up to the time of their examinations, an average of eight months after their WTC efforts ended."

A larger study released in 2006 found that roughly 70 percent of nearly 10,000 workers tested at Mount Sinai from 2002 to 2004 reported that they had new or substantially worsened respiratory problems while or after working at ground zero. This study showed that many of the respiratory ailments, including sinusitis and asthma, and gastrointestinal problems related to them, initially reported by ground zero workers persisted or grew worse over time. Most of the ground zero workers in the study who reported trouble breathing while working there were still having those problems two and a half years later, an indication of chronic illness unlikely to improve over time.

In all of these actions and decisions, President George W. Bush has acted in a manner contrary to his trust as President, and subversive of constitutional government, to the prejudice of the cause of law and justice and to the manifest injury of the people of the United States. Wherefore, President George W. Bush, by such conduct, is guilty of an impeachable offense warranting removal from office.

Article XXXV notes

EPA's Response to the World Trade Center Collapse: Challenges, Successes, and Areas for Improvement, August 21, 2003 (Report No. 2003-P-00012). http://www.epa.gov/oig/reports/2003/WTC_report_20030821.pdf

Laurie Garrett, "EPA Misled Public on 9/11 Pollution, *Newsday*, August 23, 2003. http://www.sfgate.com/cgi-bin/article.cgi?file=/c/a/2003/08/23/MN300070.DTL

Mary Agnes Carey, "House Democrats Challenge OSHA Efforts At World Trade Site," *Congressional Quarterly*, Sept. 12, 2007. http://public.cq.com/docs/hb/hbnews110-000002583136.html

"Breathing and Mental Health Problems Widespread Among Ground Zero Rescue and Recovery Workers, *Medical News Today*, September 10, 2004. http://www.medicalnewstoday.com/articles/13174.php

Anthony DePalma, "Illness Persisting in 9/11 Workers, Big Study Finds," *New York Times*, September 6, 2006. http://www.nytimes.com/2006/09/06/nyregion/06health.html

http://www.afterdowningstreet.org/

http://www.kucinich.us/

http://www.feralhouse.com